ANIMAL

THE
BAGLEY
WRIGHT
LECTURE
SERIES

DOROTHEA LASKY

ANIMAL

WAVE BOOKS

SEATTLE AND NEW YORK

Published by Wave Books

www.wavepoetry.com

Wave Books titles are distributed to the trade by

Consortium Book Sales and Distribution

Phone: 800-283-3572 / SAN 631-760X

Library of Congress Cataloging-in-Publication Data

Names: Lasky, Dorothea, 1978– author.

Title: Animal / Dorothea Lasky.

Description: First edition. | Seattle : Wave Books, [2019]

Series: Bagley Wright lecture series

Identifiers: LCCN 2019011583 | ISBN 9781940696911 (trade paperback)

Subjects: LCSH: Poetry. | Poetics.

Classification: LCC PN1031.L34 2019 | DDC 808.1—dc23

LC record available at https://lccn.loc.gov/2019011583

Designed by Crisis

Image credits: *The Snake and the glowing eggs* (p. 66)

and *The bees flying are the sweetest bees* (p. 104)

by Dorothea Lasky. Photo on p. 124 by HB.

Printed in the United States of America

9 8 7 6 5 4 3 2 1

First Edition

FOR CAROLE LASKY

ANIMAL

AN INTRODUCTION

Every Name in History is I.

NIETZSCHE

Poems are gifts that we give to the wind. The best gift that a poet can give is to allow their *I* to be its own cool animal. An *I* that is a wild thing, a mercurial trickster that resists all definition, that is so close to a self (or the self)—and so far away from it at the same time—that the reader can't help but see a real self in it. An *I* that is a self who makes so many contradictions, who manipulates the reader and their expectations to such a degree that the reader is left feeling both full and empty after having encountered it.

In this brief compendium of four lectures, I will talk about poetry and its relationship to ghosts, colors, animals, and bees. In each of these discussions, I will be thinking of poetry at least a little through the lens of an idea I have termed the *metaphysical I*. Although the idea is never named within these lectures, it affects them, as it is the crux of my poetics. It functions as a ghost haunting this book.

The *metaphysical I* is not a new idea really, just maybe a new term. I define this *I* as a wild, lyric *I*, one that has no center and has no way to predict where it will go. An *I* that is a shapeshifter. A persona that uses unexpected language and imagery, that is inconsistent, frightening, funny, and beyond the idea of a singular self.

I started thinking about this kind of *I* because I think that oftentimes a contemporary reader of a poem will conflate the *I* of the poem with the *I* of the poet (despite the fact that we have been taught in school not to do so).

This always frustrates me. Because when we reason out genre distinctions clearly, the *I* of a poem is always a kind of performer. The *I* of a poem necessarily wears a mask and is an actor. Upon its birth it has been given the holy task of acting both like and not like its real self. Always the *I* of a poem is the main eulogist at the memorial of what it wanted immortality to be while it was still a living thing.

As readers, we know that the greatest distance possible between the *I* and its author is in a work of fiction and that the closest relationship between the *I* and its author is in a work of nonfiction. There often seems to be a moral obligation that the *I* of a nonfiction piece, such as a memoir, be 100 percent truthful. Sometimes this can have even legal ramifications, too. But no, the *I* of a poem is not the *I* as it would be in a memoir.

If you are a poet, these distances are such tricky things to consider. Should the *I* be the poet? Should it not be the poet? We poets always have to make this hard call. Knowing that even when we make an *I* so clearly not ourselves, someone will assume this *I* is us anyway. Or if they know us as live persons, they will put their idea of us on our poor little *I*, an *I* in a poem with no bodily form to buffer it, just trying to make its own way.

Federico García Lorca, in his writing on the aesthetic of *duende*, discusses how when a piece of written art is good or real, it has soul. And that a soul is a kind of demon. That a piece of art is authentic when the demonic is at play in it, when it has gone to the other world and brought a spirit back to inhabit it. And so that when you are experiencing a piece of art with *duende* in it, you will feel delight and disgust when you encounter the demonic. And that without a little demon, a poem is not a poem at all.

It makes sense. After all, without a demon, how else to make the top of your head blow right off?

There is a sense in Lorca's idea of the *duende* that a poem's persona is infinitely strong to handle this demon. That the demon becomes a live alphabet, an actual, freakish live wire that the *I* of a poem must encounter, control, manipulate, beautify, handle, and, you know, just deal with.

This *I* (not the demon, but what has to control the demon) of the *duende* is what I am concerned with most in my poetics. I am concerned with the part of the demon that has to know itself and control itself. That is so much the puffed-up essence of the personal, it can harness all fragmented senses of self and use them whenever it needs to, to go beyond the self. I am talking about an *I* that is so powerful it can truly become a universal *I*.

In this book, what I mean to distinguish in thinking about poetry is what we think of as *duende* and also what isn't *duende*. I mean to suggest that poetry could think of itself as having a new sense of the *I*. Because while *duende* is the power core of the *I*—stripped down to its essence in a sort of erasure—an *I* is the use of this power to become a trickster, a thief, a demon, a little thing, infused forever with purely the occult.

In their shapeshifterness, poems with a *metaphysical I* play with their relationship to their reader in a way that is manipulative. They do so in a way that we oftentimes refer to as *postmodern*. Although this volleying relationship has happened long before the postmodern age (which is an age I don't believe in, in case you were wondering).

Nevertheless, poems with a *metaphysical I* are postmodern in that they remove the fourth wall, the veil of safe performative distance between the persona and the reader. They make evident that the persona of the poem sees you. They may act at times as if they don't realize you are peering over their shoulder, but at some point, they let you know they know. All of this they do through an ever-changing display of human emotions, through an *I* that takes on a neverending stream of costumes to make beautiful the many moods and their hot and awful divinity, to conflate both hate and love.

Poems with a *metaphysical I* are the kind of poems that I am interested in. I myself write my own poems out of necessity, summoning as much bravado as I can. And maybe I do this because when I started writing poetry my *I* was a tiny *I* that I had to blow the root upon myself to become big.

Because we all start small. One cell, one poem, one word, one utterance into the dark. The point of it all is to go beyond that beginning, to become *something* else, whatever that poem may be.

Because we all end small, too, but that's another story.

And maybe the *I* in my own poems is still very small, but I promise you that when I'm gone, my *I* is going to be as big as this whole room.

If you are reading this, poets, here's my battle cry for you to be big, too.

Begin.

POETRY, GHOSTS, AND THE SHARED IMAGINATION

Baby hair with a woman's eyes
I can feel you watching in the night
All alone with me and we're waiting for the sunlight
When I feel cold, you warm me
And when I feel I can't go on, you come and hold me
It's you—and me—forever

HALL & OATES

THE MATERIALITY OF THE IMAGINATION

In this lecture, I will discuss the shared imagination and its ability to engage with the material world. In it, I mean to argue that the imagination is a physical space that one shares with other people in and through poetry. That in a poem we make a haunted land to mimic this haunted one, and that we populate this land with physical reality to connect this world to the next (to other ones).

When we write poems, what is important about writing them is what we create within the brains of others. This is what makes the possibility of a world past this one possible.

A belief in a material imagination is important to me as a poet, because I want to not just recreate this world through poetry. I want a neverending, generative universe that poetry can help create.

One of my favorite poems by Alice Notley goes like this:

> All my life,
> since I was ten,
> I've been waiting
> to be in
> this hell here
> with you;
> all I've ever
> wanted, and
> still do.

I first heard the poem when my friend Laura Solomon put it on a mix CD she made for me in Paris, while I was living in Boston in 2005. She put it right before a song by Amadou & Mariam called "Sénégal Fast Food," so that the Notley poem was like an introduction to the song, which, not knowing French, I thought was about a late night eating fast food in Senegal. But upon reading the translation of the lyrics to the song, I later learned was about falling in love and getting married in a rush, asking the question over and over, "What time is it in Paradise?" Rushing into the question of timelessness.

In my mind, when I heard Notley read the poem in the 1987 recording, I saw her at the St. Mark's Poetry Project, reading it to a roomful of people, telling them all, I have waited to be here with you, this chamber of poets and seers, this hell that now I am a part of forever, and by the way, it is hell after all—all this gossip and dark living. But later, I learned, too, that Notley was reading her poem "All My Life" in a real city called Buffalo, a place very charged for me with emotions. A place that is, for so many people, its own kind of hell.

Much of my belief in a material imagination has to do with my belief in ghosts and a hope and horror that they really do exist.

Even though I know that Notley speaks her poem, wherever she does, to a room full of poets, telling them that she has waited to be with them, and now she is, reading her poem, at a real poetry reading, I think she is also telling them, Here I am in the space of the imagination, where you are, too.

Poems are special because they make a space, a real space, where we can all go. This place is a city called The Imagination. It is whatever you want it to be, half-hell, half-dreamworld, half-Paradise, half-light and ashes, but poems are the special things that make it real forever.

A BELIEF IN GHOSTS

My whole life, I had an inkling that there were things like ghosts and that maybe some people were able to actually see them. But up until six summers ago, I had never actually seen a ghost.

For two summers, while teaching poetry in Europe, I slept in a haunted villa. The teachers and I had all sorts of encounters with the spirits there, but for me, seeing the ghost during my first summer there was the most important event. Nothing other than seeing a ghost has been more instrumental in my thinking about the materiality of the shared imagination and its importance in poetry.

The villa has a long history of ghosts. Legend has it that a girl's shoe was once found in the wall. A guard had quit years ago after so many sightings of a tiny girl screaming for help that he could no longer bear it. While I stayed in the villa with other teachers and friends, we all heard children running overhead in the abandoned rooms upstairs, heard screams and voices, had computers charged for no reason, locked windows that blew open, hidden pills, broken cabinets, and misplaced plastic necklaces. One teacher even channeled an angry spirit in her writing, who simply stated, "I am stuck here."

All of these experiences are things that could be explained away, but with several people experiencing them, we started to talk about them freely. When some visiting artists came to stay at the villa for a few days one summer, we shared the stories with them, too.

Most people I choose to tell about my belief in ghosts are believers or at the very least susceptible to the idea. I am careful not to tell people who are going to laugh it off or call me crazy. As a poet, I have learned to be okay with what my imagination might bring to me.

When people call other people crazy I don't get mad, I get bored. When people tell me ghosts don't exist, I just get bored.

Laura K. Leuter, a famed devil hunter who has devoted her life to looking for the physical evidence of a being lovingly called the Jersey Devil, has written of nonbelievers in her plight:

> Until someone proves that there isn't something out there, I will continue to believe that there is, and I will also continue my efforts to find proof that the Jersey Devil does in fact exist. So there.

When these visitors were at the villa, a few of us told them about the ghosts. It felt natural enough. I didn't think so much to censor myself, because the ghosts just seemed real. I have long believed (and longed to believe) what Pablo Picasso told me, that "Everything you can imagine is real."

One night a teacher and I arrived home late from dinner. We heard someone (or something) calling to us from the lemon garden right outside the villa. I thought I heard, "Dottie, come here." We got very scared and ran in the villa, clutching our neon leather purses to our chests.

We talked each other into going back out and seeing who was there. "Who is there! Who is there!" my friend shrieked. We heard, "It is Hortense."

Hortense was an old owner of the villa. We walked into the garden with shaky knees only to find not the apparition of Hortense, but the visiting artists laughing at us. I didn't find it funny.

One of the visitors (let's call him Demon from now on) proceeded to tell me I needed to see a psychiatrist. After about two minutes, I realized I wasn't going to be able to control my anger in any sort of good way, so I went inside, happy to be in the arms of the real ghosts in my room, not among the placid thoughts of living demons.

Samuel Johnson said of ghosts:

> It is wonderful that five thousand years have now elapsed since the creation of the world, and still it is undecided whether or not there has ever been an instance of the spirit of any person appearing after death. All argument is against it; but all belief is for it.

All arguments, logical and steeped in what we know of science, can easily refute any belief in ghosts. The most salient argument that ghost-believers have is that they have "seen one." And the imaginative space of a being having seen *something*—let alone a dead spirit—is not something that we ever fully believe in. But why not?

As a poet, I think a lot about belief, the belief in what my mind might bring to me. There are a lot of things that enter my mind that I choose to translate into language. All poems contain images and these images have been in the poet's brain and hang in the balance always, to be given to the reader upon reading. And in a poem images have weight, so that you cannot help but believe in them.

Emily Dickinson said of belief:

> On subjects of which we know nothing . . . we both believe, and disbelieve a hundred times an Hour, which keeps Believing nimble.

The thing about ghosts is that once they have entered your imaginative space, there is no way not to believe in them. As I mentioned, I once actually saw a ghost.

THE SIGHTING OF THE GHOST

The poet John Wieners wrote, "I can only say real happiness yields from the world of poems. And its practitioners are secret, sacred vessels to an ancient divinity."

As I mentioned before, I think poetry is special because it connects us to the imagination, another world, or perhaps *the* other world, which is a physical space that poems interact with and encounter.

In his 1940 book *The Imaginary*, Sartre writes that when a writer creates something, they have "visions" and that these visions are made into a very real space in the brain.

Sartre's idea seems to me very much in line with what Dickinson writes of in her poem about death:

> After great pain, a formal feeling comes –
> The Nerves sit ceremonious, like Tombs –
> The stiff Heart questions 'was it He, that bore,'
> And 'Yesterday, or Centuries before'?

> The Feet, mechanical, go round –
> A Wooden way
> Of Ground, or Air, or Ought –
> Regardless grown,
> A Quartz contentment, like a stone –
>
> This is the Hour of Lead –
> Remembered, if outlived,
> As Freezing persons, recollect the Snow –
> First – Chill – then Stupor – then the letting go –

As Dickinson writes, when a person dies, after pain, comes the "formal feeling" of cold, to let go of the person as a being, to release them into a space where all voices commingle, as "Freezing persons, recollect the Snow." To have a vision of a feeling is a type of formality. Perhaps poets are the beings on this earth that can go into the freezing place and bring out the pieces of snow. Something that Bernadette Mayer appropriated for her translation of Catullus #48, something she describes as a "formal field of kissing," of being in love, a place where one kiss is never enough, where one kiss is just never enough snow.

I think the formal field is the land of light and ashes, a place of visions, a place, as Jack Spicer wrote about in his lecture "Dictation and 'A Textbook of Poetry,'" that the dead speak from and a poet receives radio messages from, a place which might be an "Outside, . . . an id down in the cortex which you can't reach anyway, . . . galaxies which seem to be sending radio messages to us with the whole of the galaxy blowing up just to say something to us."

In comparing himself rather snarkily to Byron, Keats wrote, "He describes what he sees—I describe what I imagine—Mine is the hardest task."

I tend to agree with him.

When I got to the villa the first year, I couldn't sleep for about two weeks. Maybe I slept an hour or two here and there. I couldn't sleep because I felt certain something was in the room with me.

It sounds crazy to say all of this to you, I know, but after a while I started talking to the presence in my room. In words, in my imaginative space, she spoke back.

We communicated.

She conveyed who she was and that she liked my jewelry and just wanted to hang out sometimes. This made sense—I mean, have you seen my jewelry? Also, because I would often see my jewelry pop up in odd places, after I had locked it away in a drawer or cabinet. She told me she had lived in the sixteenth century. In my mind, I had the vision of her as a teenager with long blond hair. I was absolutely certain that this is what she looked like.

For fear of seeming crazy, I didn't tell anyone about our communication. But once it happened, I felt free and slept like a baby.

A few days later, my student told me that she had something important to tell me. She said that when she was in the workout room the night before, a sort of creepy-looking blond teenager tried to turn off her treadmill, but that when she went to touch the girl's hand and implore the girl to stop, the hand and the girl disappeared into the air.

I told my student about my encounter with what was likely this same entity. We both felt better. We shared a belief in another dimension of being. And we had both interacted with the same ghost. There was a comfort in this shared reality, this shared imagination.

This is probably the opposite of how one should feel in that situation. Were we both going insane? Did we both have heatstroke? Did we prove that ghosts exist? Still, it was something very special that our brains connected in this way, with this same image.

Up until this point, I hadn't actually seen the ghost. Despite my wanting to believe, I've always kind of not believed in ghosts, too, and never having seen one made me feel slightly disconnected from them.

The morning after my student shared her story with me, I came back to the villa from a trip to town. As I walked to my room in the early morning heat, I saw a teenager, about one hundred feet from me in the olive grove. The girl had on periwinkle shorts, a particular shade my mother had gotten into in the '80s. (In my mind, I can see a stack of periwinkle sweaters piled on her bed now.) The girl was not so much wearing shorts, as a skort. She was looking at the leaves of a tree, as if she were looking for something. Curious, but partially with the manner of a scientist. I thought she was one of my students, so I looked down. I didn't feel like talking to anyone. A few seconds later, feeling guilty (aren't teachers supposed to *always* be ready to talk to students?), I looked up. The girl was gone. I blinked. There was no way a person could have gotten away so fast. "That's odd," I said aloud to myself.

Only later that day, when I revisited the memory, did I remember she had gleaming blond hair.

Only months later did I think of one of my favorite moments of Stanley Kubrick's 1980 film, *The Shining*, when Scatman Crothers's character, Dick Hallorann, explains to Danny, the psychic boy, that the images in the haunted hotel are like pictures in a book, and that they aren't real. Danny repeats this to himself when he sees the ghosts of the hotel: "Remember what Mr. Hallorann said. It's just like pictures in a book, Danny. It isn't real."

It is not important to me to try and figure out if what I saw was "real" or an apparition. What I had sensed through my eyes had been processed into my brain as material space, in that what may have been a real image of my ghost had weight in my brain. It took up space in my brain.

Sometimes we see things in life very fast, so fast that we doubt ourselves, but we still know they are there. For example, oftentimes when we have mice in our kitchen (or is it just me?), they flash by, giving us a split second to register what they are. How often we can doubt what we saw, but still we have evidence to know what was there.

In the case of mice, there are droppings, broken bread crumbs, bananas with bite marks. With ghosts, there are often residues that are imperceptible, existing wholly within the imagination. With love, isn't it love that we have felt, even when the physical reality has passed? Still, love is felt so clearly and neverendingly without sometimes so much as a sight of the beloved. We don't need to see or touch a person to love them until the day we die. Just ask someone who has lost a person they have loved to refute this.

POETRY NEEDS A BELIEF IN A MATERIAL IMAGINATION

You can't always see what you hold in your imagination, but imagination is deeply felt.

Poetry has the ability to have us interact with the imaginary, because words together in the space of a poem make new realities—they make all the illusions of the imaginary real through language.

In his book *The Double Flame*, in an essay called "The Kingdoms of Pan," Octavio Paz explains that poetry is always about an embodied imagination, making the unreal, the almost real, actually real:

> When we dream and when we couple, we embrace phantoms. Each of the two who constitute the couple possesses a body, a face, and a name, but their real reality, precisely at the most intense moment of the embrace, disperses in a cascade of sensation which disperses in turn. There is a question that all lovers ask each other, and in it the erotic mystery is epitomized: Who are you? A question without an answer . . . The senses are and are not of this world. By means of them, poetry traces a bridge between *seeing* and *believing*. By that bridge, imagination is embodied and bodies turn into images.

And while any kind of thinking makes the imagination embodied, it is the holy space of a poet's projected imagination, a space where new language can create new worlds, that does so most poignantly.

Many years ago, as my father was suffering from Alzheimer's, which he later died from, he would often go into a trance and say that he had been talking to his brother and father, who had both died decades earlier. Everyone around us, all the doctors and nurses, said it was a psychotic break of the disease, that what he thought he saw was the residue of his long-term memory, breaking down and making him think the past was the present. They would give him a drug like Abilify, and he would quiet down. But who is to say that he didn't see his brother again? Who is to say that his long-term memory wasn't a thing being eroded away by the disease, but a space he was visiting, which he could visit again, one day soon, for an eternity?

In the 1965 lecture I mentioned earlier, Jack Spicer wrote of Yeats's wife Georgie's encounter with the spirits, how on one particular occasion she got possessed by spirits and Yeats was able to speak directly to them. When Yeats asked them, "What are you here for?" they spoke to him through her and said, "We're here to give metaphors for your poetry." A generous set of ghosts that knew Yeats. But I think that all spirits in the spirit world are generous, when you meet them in the space of the Imagination within a poem.

DOES A MATERIAL IMAGINATION MAKE A VISIONARY POETRY

I am not the only poet to have ever actually seen an apparition.

Many years ago, I remember reading an anthology of sorts on visionary poets. In the book, there was a story of Blake and how he saw angels in the trees, as a kind of physical reality of angels. When we see, we perceive that the thing we see has weight, especially if it is a person-like thing, like an angel. To have a vision of something, to perceive in a visionary way, is to assume in some way that what we see is real, or weighty, is affected by gravity, is material. Blake saw the angel, believed that he saw it, and it changed him. It created a space in his mind for the angel to go. He wrote poems about it, with new words and new language and new angels from this imaginative space. We read those poems still.

My favorite scene from *The Shining* has always been when Jack Torrance, the murderous father, goes to visit room 237, the most haunted room in the whole hotel. For many reasons—most of them lifted from the recent documentary *Room 237*, in which theorist Jay Weidner asserts that the movie is Kubrick's confession of how he helped to fake the moon-landing films—this room is always what I think of now as "The Moon Room."

After Jack goes into the room, there are very slow shots as he travels up the space. The camera focuses on the loud and beautiful purple-

and-green carpet, with its radiating phalluses, the neon lilac couches, black-and-white bedspread and very mundane hotel wallpaper. Although slightly stylized, the room feels very real and deeply felt.

Next, he finds himself in the mint-green and gold bathroom, where he encounters the ghost of a murdered woman. She is in the bath, and slowly pulls back the slightly opaque shower curtain to reveal her body, naked and statuesque. She gets out of the tub and moves toward him. She sees him.

I was recently on a tour in a very old museum with many portraits. The guide, an art historian, talked about how we might have a portrait on the wall today and think nothing of it, but in the past people kept cloaks or cloth over their portraits. It was thought that a portrait or art object was not something that you should look upon daily, because the act of seeing, of vision, was bidirectional, so that when you looked at something, it looked back at you, and changed you.

I think in this way that a vision has viscera. That the bidirectionality of the seeing one to the thing being seen means that all vision and imaginative space created between the two things has weight.

When the ghost in room 237 looks at Jack, she starts to charm and mesmerize him. He becomes transfixed by the eroticism of the scene and forgets the possibility that she isn't a living being, that her image isn't real. She uses the bidirectionality of their interaction to get him to move toward her. It is more than mere seduction between ghost and living being. It is the magnetic pull of faith that he has in his imagination through either his erotic feelings, her supernatural allure, or her intent. It is a mix of this magic spell.

Everyone knows how this scene ends. As he kisses her, she reveals herself to be an old crone, then a corpse, and laughs at his faith in his own stupidity. Still, even in her decay, she is deeply felt in our imaginative spaces. She exists as some force. We see her and hear her as she chases him out. There is a materiality to her presence, whether only in Jack's mind or our minds now. Still, she exists there, in some dimension, in some version of real space and time.

Søren Kierkegaard, in his 1843 *Fear and Trembling*, discusses three levels of perception of the realms of being: aesthetic/sensual, moral, and spiritual. He believes that most people go the three-step path—an aesthetic or sensual experience leads to a moral understanding, which leads to an interaction with the spiritual world. He argues that the aesthetic/sensual, when done right, takes a person right up to the spiritual realm. That when we make a truly beautiful piece of art, we make a fast train into the land of specters.

When a poem happens, meaning and a shared imagination happen between a poet and a reader. The poem is the testimony. The poet and reader are in mental and aesthetic—and then spiritual—communion.

WHAT ABOUT REALITY THAT IS NOT REAL, WHAT ABOUT POETRY

I have always loved the poem "Song of a Man Who Has Come Through" by D. H. Lawrence:

> Not I, not I, but the wind that blows through me!
> A fine wind is blowing the new direction of Time.
> If only I let it bear me, carry me, if only it carry me!
> If only I am sensitive, subtle, oh, delicate, a winged gift!
> If only, most lovely of all, I yield myself and am borrowed
> By the fine, fine wind that takes its course through the chaos of the world

Like a fine, an exquisite chisel, a wedge-blade inserted;
If only I am keen and hard like the sheer tip of a wedge
Driven by invisible blows,
The rock will split, we shall come at the wonder, we shall find the
    Hesperides.

Oh, for the wonder that bubbles into my soul,
I would be a good fountain, a good well-head,
Would blur no whisper, spoil no expression.

What is the knocking?
What is the knocking at the door in the night?
It is somebody wants to do us harm.

No, no, it is the three strange angels.
Admit them, admit them.

There is a lot to say about this poem, but, of course, what I have always loved the most about it are the "three strange angels." Who are they?

The word "strange" doesn't really tell us much about who these angels are, but it gives us enough to know that they aren't of this world, that they are part of the imagination.

Sometimes I think (and it isn't exactly a new thought!) that when we write poetry, we always engage with ghosts. Maybe what we perceive quickly is what poetry collects for us, a space of half impressions, of sensual residues. And maybe the things we only see or feel for an instant are the spaces of nonreality—superreality—coming into this world.

Is this maybe what Alice Notley meant when she wrote that all her life, since she was ten, she had been waiting to be in this hell here with us?

Is the living within the real but a radio connection to a peaceful world of specters, what for Blake was the hell of reality in his "Book of Thel," where he had to ask, "Why a little curtain of flesh on the bed of our desire?" His question has haunted me all *my* life. Snow snow.

Surely the ghost in room 237 is part of the imagination, part of Jack's and now part of ours. Or was her presence a weighted thing always. Is there a space somewhere, where room 237 exists and she does, too? And does she touch Jack over and over again and make him run away, on a loop? And will we meet her, too, in another time or place, because she has been born within our brains and will live there forever, a constant loop of imaginative memory?

Did the blond ghost bless me with the knowledge that the unseen is real, an openness to a door where other ghosts can pass through? Or did the blond ghost make a crack in my sanity that may never be reglued? Did she make it impossible for me to ever see reality as wholly palpable again?

What seems most important about the event is how my student and I both shared her image. How much did our tellings and retellings of our encounters change her and change our memories of her and make her alive? Alive at once or alive again—isn't it all the same thing?

THE PRACTICE OF MATHEMATICS

To conclude, I bring in William Blake's *Newton*, an image of a person bent over his studies, his eyes focused on his theorem and not on the world around him. To me, he has always looked so much like a poet. Sitting with his back bent, the burden of gravity and language and light —and the night—upon him.

Perhaps an interpretation of this image is that the mathematician is so obsessed with the abstraction of reality that he can't see the beauty of the world around him. That maybe he sees only with, not through, the eye, because he thinks, and does not experience, the world.

Still, I can't help but think that this image is about the materiality of the imagination. That Blake's Mathematician or Poet makes a space with his paper where other thinkers can go, a space where we all can dare to go.

In a show a few years ago at the Whitney Museum of American Art, I watched a movie of Ken Jacobs's Apparition Theater of New York, which required 3-D glasses. Among other images, one part of the theater was a group of shadows playing with balloons, and at one point, a sign went up that said, "Balloons go into the audience and you can't tell what's real." Even though I knew they were not real balloons, I held my hands out to catch them as they bounded toward me. It was the magic of wanting to see the boundary between the real and unreal dissolved. To see the curtain of flesh on the bed of my desire lifted once more.

The imagination is a space where things can go. Where we make things up and share them with others. But the imagination is not a vortex to suck the world up, like the annihilation of death. The imagination is a holy space where things can live forever.

Maxine Greene, in her *Releasing the Imagination*, writes:

> The way things are for our life and body allows us only a partial view of things, not the kind of total view we might gain if we were godlike, looking down from the sky. But we can only know as situated beings. We see aspects of objects and people around us; we all live in [a] kind of incompleteness . . . and there is always more for us to see.
>
> Once again, this is where imagination enters in, as the felt possibility of looking beyond the boundary where the backyard ends or the road narrows, diminishing out of sight.

I once had a dream—I don't remember the details—but I remember I woke up and I shot up in bed and said, "Maybe they give you the flowers in a different way. That's poetry."

There is a consciousness among humans—and likely all animals, maybe all living things, but most definitely humans—that we can share. We share the material imagination through poetry.

Alice Notley wrote in a recent poem, "Last night I saw that when I flowed out and became all else I was nothing, / I was everything. We are the electricity."

And as Carl Sagan said, "We are made of starstuff."

We are the starstuff. We are the electricity, the hope of the balloons bounding toward us, the holy holograms. This reality may be a violent one, but isn't it the case that we will all be glad to know one another forever through poetry? To always choose "one root of the white sort" over a million blue-violets. To be in the hell and the heaven of the space of the imagination. To take a chance that this space is there and make this life the immortal one.

If you love someone and they die, make them come alive again in a poem.

Read a poem again, and the dead don't have to be gone. I promise you this much.

Think of it another way. Read a poem. Then you won't have to be gone one day, too.

To hell and back again: I send you.

WHAT IS COLOR IN POETRY OR IS IT THE WILD WIND IN THE SPACE OF THE WORD

"It's more like a corkscrew than a path!"
LEWIS CARROLL, *Through the Looking-Glass*

NOT A PATH, BUT A CORKSCREW

I cite Lewis Carroll to begin this lecture, because I found this quotation in a book called *The Rainbow Book: A Collection of Essays & Illustrations Devoted to Rainbows in Particular & Spectral Sequences in General.* This 1975 color compendium is devoted to thinking about the meaning behind our visible spectrum and has, in many ways, inspired this entire lecture. It is an important book to me because I spied it at Joshua Beckman's house several years ago, and it was as if a dormant light was turned on once again.

I think when Joshua saw me and my sleeping light all lit up, he was afraid I would steal his book, knowing how much I think about color and poetry. I must confess that I didn't steal it, but that I thought about it and, after I left his house, had to run online and buy two copies for myself.

Within *The Rainbow Book*, the Carroll quotation begins a discussion of the gyre, the idea that Yeats was fond of at least in part, that time is not a linear path, but a swirling spectrum of events and occurrences. I think our idea that the color spectrum is a linear construct is just as faulty as our idea that time is one. Poems know this, that neither time, nor visible color, nor being, falls down a straight path. What is meaning if not something you can't find in a neat set of steps? A poem is special because its logic is emotional and aesthetic and resists the traditional ways logic seeks to jail itself. Color is special because there is no way to pin it down. It has a live wire that illuminates its frequency. Of course, a poem does, too.

I digress a good bit already. I mean to tell you now, before I totally begin, that this lecture will explore the relationships between color and poetry. It will delve into some ideas by color theorists, as well as discuss specific poems that use color "well." It will also give gentle suggestions for where future poetry can start to go in using color in new ways.

In the spirit of disclosure, I must tell you that this lecture has taken many forms over the past year. I have written parts of it, abandoned it, and then taken it up again. In preparing for this lecture last winter and then over the summer, I reached an impasse of thinking, starting one draft and then starting up again. The topic is bigger than I could ever even begin to discuss today. And in throwing all my colors into the wind over several months, I wrote this simple couplet one day in my notes to begin again:

I love color
And that is all that I love

It may be that this really is the truth. I have always loved color. I always forget what my mother's being a painter might mean to me and the lens with which I read poetry. I recently told some friends casually that my mother was a painter and art historian, and one of them, the wonderful poet Emily Pettit, said well, it all makes sense, that's why you love color.

It's true that my house growing up was always ablaze with color, bright objects and paint everywhere. Every vacation involved either purchasing an art object or visiting a museum. Color was our religion. My mother hung Navajo rugs in almost every room, and when I close my eyes to this day I see the pulse of the bright red, orange, and teal triangles of our living room eye-dazzler.

All families have big issues that they discuss constantly. Our big issue was color. Instead of baseball or politics, my mother and I talked a lot about what made a particular object come alive.

One lifelong family discussion was about a wooden rocking chair my mother made and stained for me when I was two. She asked me what color I wanted it stained: red or blue. I chose blue clearly, but she thought to herself, what toddler has that kind of color preference? As I was growing up, being the pain in the ass that I was, this was always a point of contention for me, and I always found reason to bring it up: "That red rocking tiny rocking chair should have been blue!" I'd exclaim whenever I was in a bad mood. When I was a teenager, we had a choice between a red or blue lounge chair and, of course, blue finally won its due.

When I first started writing poems, around age seven, I would memorize them and recite them to anyone who would listen. One I would always recite was called "Blue Dignity," so I will share it with you now, because hey, why not, you are all here to listen to me:

Blue dignity
Is suddenly black

And brown and grey
Other colors that cause flack

A sapphire poses
Amongst a bed of roses

And strength and triumph remain
Where graceful refrain

Oh copper-colored cream
What did I dream

Don't replay the past
Or snakes will wrath

Violets violets of the sea
Why did you

Leave me

Perhaps because of this personal history, I can't help but see that color has a kind of bidirectional meaning making, especially with art and everyday objects. You can choose what color the objects are, and this choice makes meaning upon them and then changes what meaning you put upon them. Choosing an object's color is much like naming a baby. You can find the right thing, hopefully. You can paint, restain, reupholster. Color is a malleable thing, based on mood, on time. Color can change or can stay the same and react to people and its environment. In this way, color is a live wire.

When you read poems that get color right, there are a million possibilities of what that color could be, but there's a certainty that the color the poet chose is correct among a million different possibilities. When poems get color right, there is a kind of color fate to the pairing between the visible and energetic frequency of the word, and the sound of the word.

Perhaps Rimbaud got the connection between color and language best in his poem "Vowels," which sets out to illustrate a colored alphabet within a poem. A translation by Paul Schmidt and Peter Bauer goes like this:

> Black A, white E, red I, green U, blue O—vowels,
> Some day I will open your silent pregnancies:
> A, black belt, hairy with bursting flies,
> Bumbling and buzzing over stinking cruelties.
>
> Pits of night; E, candor of sand and pavilions,
> High glacial spears, white kings, trembling Queen-Anne's lace;
> I, bloody spittle, laughter dribbling from a face
> In wild denial or in anger, vermilions;
>
> U, . . . divine movement of viridian seas,
> Peace of pastures animal-strewn, peace of calm lines
> Drawn on foreheads worn with heavy alchemies;
>
> O, supreme Trumpet, harsh with strange stridencies,
> Silences traced in angels and astral designs:
> O . . . OMEGA . . . the violet light of His Eyes!

In this poem, Rimbaud sends up the one-to-one correspondence between a progression of letters as a progression of time and a life, a correspondence that Edmond Jabès talks about in *The Book of Questions* (Volume II):

> The letters of the alphabet are contemporaries of death. They are stages of death turned into signs. Death of eternal death. But there are other signs which the letters covet, erased signs reproduced by gestures at the heart of what is named. Thus the bird's take-off contains all forms of flight. And is it not also the bird which, as it cuts through the sky, writes and repeats the universal "delete" which rules our fate? Ah, the written world dies and is reborn of the bird.

Perhaps to name a letter is to name a color, too. It is to set a finite progression of colors and letters and things that fold upon each other in the voraciously eating vortex of time. That is not a corkscrew but a path. That is all moments, all colors, letters, all forms of flight. That is the dormant light all lit up.

Perhaps when we connect color to language, to sound, in the space of a poem, we reconnect and resist what André Breton has described as the tragic bifurcation of the so-called real and dream worlds that happens to all adults. Perhaps this is poetry's purpose in our lives, to reconnect the real and dream worlds to one's own dormant light. Of course, I believe the easiest way to do this with language is through the perfect use of color.

WHAT OF IMAGE, WHAT OF COLOR

I have always thought that H.D.'s poems are so perfect because they focus closely on images and make sure that her picture of whatever she mentions in her poem is shared completely with her reader. Take, for example, her poem "Sea Violet":

> The white violet
> is scented on its stalk,
> the sea-violet

fragile as agate,
lies fronting all the wind
among the torn shells
on the sand-bank.

The greater blue violets
flutter on the hill,
but who would change for these
who would change for these
one root of the white sort?

Violet
your grasp is frail
on the edge of the sand-hill,
but you catch the light—
frost, a star edges with its fire.

The sea-violet, described so well—over and over again, turned over again and again, to be peered at from many angles by the reader—becomes part of a shared imagination with the reader. By the end of the poem, H.D. and the reader share the image of the sea-violet, its gorgeous white flower body embodied as imaginative reality in both of their minds.

Part of H.D.'s achievement has to do with her keen use of color. The white of the sea-violet and the blue of the other violets serve to distinguish both sorts so simply and so dramatically. This drama echoes what fellow Imagist, Ezra Pound, wrote about in his 1918 "A Retrospect" that "good poetry" has "Direct treatment of the 'thing' whether subjective or objective" and "absolutely no word that does not contribute to the presentation."

We can see in this poem that each word was chosen precisely and that her use of colors allows her to achieve a great deal with very little language, so that there is no excess that "does not contribute." It is the perfect choice of colors that makes the shared imagination (the shared imaginative space, in material) of the reader and the poet, at least in part and for one second in communion. The violets in H.D.'s poem have been agreed upon between poet and reader, at least in part, because of their colors.

H.D. famously called herself the modern Sappho, and part of her love of Sappho seems to be her love of Sappho's use of colors. If you have ever read Sappho, particularly Anne Carson's gorgeous translation (2003), you know how vividly Sappho used the colors violet and yellow, and how they figure in constant vibration with each other, due to their complementary natures. Sappho writes, for example, of "the one with violets in her lap," of "having come from heaven wrapped in a purple cloak," and of "Dawn with gold sandals."

In her essay "The Wise Sappho," H.D. writes:

> Impassioned roses are dead.
>
> "Little, but all roses"—true there is a tint of rich colour (invariably we find it), violets, purple woof of cloth, scarlet garments, dyed fastening of a sandal, the lurid, crushed and perished hyacinth, stains on cloth and flesh and parchment.
>
> There is gold too. Was it a gold rose the poet meant? . . .
>
> I think of the words of Sappho as these colours, or states rather, transcending colour yet containing (as great heat the compass of the spectrum) all colour.

Color is a kind of conduit that connects the spiritual and material worlds. As H.D. writes, this means that when color in a poem is used to great effect it becomes "transcending colour . . . containing . . . [the] (great heat the compass of the spectrum) all colour."

What I am trying to say here, though, is that color is not simply a decorative element in a poem. Color makes an expanse—a field, a shared formal field, with which to plant more shared components of the material imagination—a poem. Color makes this space bigger, this imaginative space more specific and bigger, and gives it weight. Color makes this expanse—a colorless idea—into something solid.

Recently, I learned about the Pirahã society in Brazil. It is said that the Pirahã have no specific words for colors like the ones I am talking about here. So, whereas if we were to describe a red flower, someone who is part of Pirahã might describe the color of it as "the thing that is like blood." Likewise, a blond girl's hair might be described as "the thing that is like the sun."

Even without specific color words, people can communicate the tone and weight of a color through language. It is not about the magic of a word for color. It is about the magic of sharing the weighted imaginative space between speaker and listener that a description of color can produce. To describe a thing's color is to make the energy of it change.

In "Very Strong February," Bernadette Mayer changes the energy of the poem each time she changes the color in each new line:

> A man and a woman pretend to be white ice
> Three men at the lavender door are closed in by the storm
> With strong prejudice and money to buy the green pines
> One weekend fisherman and blue painters watch
> The vivid violet winds blow visibility from the mountain
> Beyond the black valley. That means or then you know
> You're in a big cloud of it, it's brilliant white mid-February
> A week or two left on distracting black trees
> Before the brownish buds obscure your view of the valley again.

Looking for company four dark men and a burnt sienna woman
Come in for three minutes, then bye-bye like a gold watch left on the
chair
Or part of the sum of what big white families think up
To store for long yellow Sundays to eat for brown ecological company.
At some point later gorgeous red adventure stops, did you forget
To turn it down and laugh in the face of the fearful white storm anyway
Or picture it brilliant blue for a further Sunday memory
In a coloring book, you talk as lightly as you can
Refusing a big pink kiss, you burned the Sunday sauce
Of crushed red tomatoes, you turn it down to just an orange glow.
This particular storm, considering the pause and the greenish thaw
before it
Reminds me in its mildness of imitating a sea-green memory that is
actually
In the future, I imitate an imagined trumpet sound
Or the brilliant purple words of a man or woman I haven't met yet
Or perhaps it's a grey-haired man I already know who said something
yesterday
To a mutual friend who will give me the whole story in black and white
tomorrow
Or the day after, just as the big orange plows for the local businesses
Go to work to push away the rest of the white snow that will fall tonight.

Almost every line in her poem includes a color. I often think: What would this poem be without these colors? How would it contain its material reality without them?

For example, what is the *black* in "A week or two left on distracting black trees"? Without it the line would be "A week or two left on distracting trees." Without black, the trees are regular green and brown trees. What is the *pink* in "Refusing a big pink kiss, you burned the Sunday sauce"? The bursting warmth of a pink kiss influencing the warm color of a Sunday tomato sauce in our imaginations. Without it, the line would be "Refusing a big kiss, you burned the Sunday sauce." In this colorless line, the sauce could be any color, a burned-out one and not as sexy and warm.

What about the line, "Or the brilliant purple words of a man or woman I haven't met yet"? Without *purple* adding a touch of royalty and strangeness to the words, the line would simply be, "Or the brilliant words of a man or woman I haven't met yet." Brilliant, noncolor words that are flat and meaningless.

It is the colors in Mayer's poem that take it from a didactic explanation of a series of meaningless, everyday events into the spectral space of the poet's imagination, a bidirectional kind of looking between Mayer and us in the space of the poem. A multifaceted meaning-making machine. Or a poem, as they call it.

So that when we use color in a poem, it is not an abstract state, but an association that has weight, that is tangible. A translation of reality, but again, what is reality? Is it the wild wind in the space of the word? The connection between the dream and the non-dream (and is this the waking). A poem helps us know.

In Mayer's poem, color creates a kind of imaginative testimony. Both the poet and the reader are part of its testimony through the use of color and the way the color changes reality.

Georg Trakl is a poet who creates a hallucinatory world through his mix of natural imagery and unnatural (or supernatural) color, reconnecting the real and dream worlds. Take for instance his poem "An Evening":

In the evening the sky was overcast.
And through the grove full of silence and grief
A dark-golden shower went.
Distant evening bells faded away.

The earth has drunk icy water,
At the forest's edge a fire lay glowing,
The wind quietly sang with angel's voices
And shivering I have gone to the knee,

In the heather, in bitter cresses.
Far outside clouds swam in silver puddles,
Desolate guards of love.
The heath was lonesome and unmeasured.

In Trakl's poem, "the earth" does something it can't really do, as it "has drunk icy water." The forest is edged in fire, not its natural color, like a darker brown or green. The clouds become inverted and turn into "silver puddles." The rain is not clear water but a "dark-golden shower." There is a quiet hallucinatory quality to the poem, which in lots of ways is so disturbing, due largely in part to color choice that quietly creates a shared supernatural imagination between poet and reader. A poet such as Rimbaud writes poems that are loud with their effect on the world, they have a louder register, but Trakl quietly changes the natural world and the imaginative space in the poem, in the minds of poet and reader.

Color in a poem can change the shared imaginative space the poem creates. It can make a new reality, with the imperceptible coming into reality—completely terrifying—as in Wallace Stevens's poem "Disillusionment of Ten O'Clock," where he embodies disembodied nightgowns with hallucinatory color choices:

The houses are haunted
By white night-gowns.
None are green,
Or purple with green rings,
Or green with yellow rings,
Or yellow with blue rings.
None of them are strange,
With socks of lace
And beaded ceintures.
People are not going
To dream of baboons and periwinkles.
Only, here and there, an old sailor,
Drunk and asleep in his boots,
Catches tigers
In red weather.

Stevens uses lots of colors with simple color names (*white, green*), although he throws a gorgeous blurple like *periwinkle* in there. Still, he hints at the multiplicity of reality, at the effect of color on reality, with his "purple with green rings" and "yellow with blue rings," which produce the unfamiliar/familiar feeling of the spiritual realm, the actual weirdness and awe of the ghosts that haunt the houses in their "white night-gowns" with nightgowns that are unexpectedly also somehow not white, and the sad and drunk old sailor caught in a neverending world of "red weather." The poem also seems very concerned about the fact that in a colorless reality, people's imaginations aren't ignited, that "People are not going / To dream of baboons and periwinkles." They will only dream of an old sailor (the poor guy!), here and there, not the fantastical blue-purple baboons and beyond.

In Stevens's "Domination of Black," we see color within the absence of color names:

At night, by the fire,
The colors of the bushes
And of the fallen leaves,
Repeating themselves,
Turned in the room,
Like the leaves themselves
Turning in the wind.
Yes: but the color of the heavy hemlocks
Came striding.
And I remembered the cry of the peacocks.

The colors of their tails
Were like the leaves themselves
Turning in the wind,
In the twilight wind.
They swept over the room,
Just as they flew from the boughs of the hemlocks
Down to the ground.
I heard them cry—the peacocks.
Was it a cry against the twilight
Or against the leaves themselves
Turning in the wind,
Turning as the flames
Turned in the fire,
Turning as the tails of the peacocks
Turned in the loud fire,
Loud as the hemlocks

Full of the cry of the peacocks?
Or was it a cry against the hemlocks?

Out of the window,
I saw how the planets gathered
Like the leaves themselves
Turning in the wind.
I saw how the night came,
Came striding like the color of the heavy hemlocks
I felt afraid.
And I remembered the cry of the peacocks.

In "Domination of Black," the only color Stevens uses is the color *black* in the title. After that color becomes the word *color*. This poem is a perfect example of what happens when a poet decides to precisely not include the perfect color name to incite our imaginative landscapes, and to suggest it through its absence. We are up to our own devices to imagine the vibrancy of the colors of the hemlocks and peacocks against the dominating black. The rhyming sound of them is a way to connect them, both multicolored and still full of complementary colors in the dominating lipstick-red of the hemlock berry and the green-blue hues of the peacock's feathers. It is through the sound and absence of color that Stevens paints a poem full of colors through the stark and overbearing black. Their absence ignites them in our imaginations.

Color is not the only sensual detail a poet can use to create a shared imagination with his or her reader. But it is an overwhelming one. One that accesses the shared imagination swiftly and, often, completely.

In his *Theory of Colours* (1810), Goethe writes:

> It will be more intelligible to assert that a dormant light resides in the eye, and that it may be excited by the slightest cause from within or from without. In darkness we can, by an effort of imagination, call up the brightest images; in dreams objects appear to us as in broad daylight; awake, the slightest external action of light is perceptible, and if the organ suffers an actual shock, light and colours spring forth.

I love this idea that even in the absence of light, our imagination is readily capable of producing it in dreams. That the imagination houses a dormant light. I think that poets and writers have very strong dormant lights just waiting to be shared. Sometimes I think that if all poets used their dormant lights extensively, it would have a viral effect, and the brains of all of us would be even more lit up.

Wittgenstein, in his 1950 *Remarks on Colour*, gives poets a charge, in explaining that we can often describe colors more accurately in words than we can recreate them. As he writes:

> 256. To be able generally to name a colour, is not the same as being able to copy it exactly. I can perhaps say "There I see a reddish place" and yet I can't mix a colour that I recognize as being exactly the same.
>
> 257. Try, for example, to paint what you see when you close your eyes! And yet you can *roughly* describe it.

Although his points are arguable, they are exciting ideas to consider. Maybe the purpose of poems is also to reconnect the real and dream worlds, to light our dormant lights to describe the infinite colors that are impossible to perfectly recreate in the natural world. Maybe that is somehow the point and the purpose of being a poet, to describe what can't ever be again.

CERTAIN COLORS AND THE VIOLET SUN: A RED HAT AND BLUE, AND RED AND BLUE

One strain of my interest in color and poetry started thirteen years ago with my love of a poem called "A Red Hat," by Gertrude Stein, from her 1914 *Tender Buttons*. It reads:

> A dark grey, a very dark grey, a quite dark grey is monstrous ordinarily, it is so monstrous because there is no red in it. If red is in everything it is not necessary. Is that not an argument for any use of it and even so is there any place that is better, is there any place that has so much stretched out.

I first read that poem in the fall right after college when I had already spent the summer thinking almost exclusively about the color red paired with the color aquamarine. I kept imagining making a necklace of aquamarines with one single bright red bead. The fantasy transcended into other mental images where red might be a singular thing in a sea of paler attributes. I imagined a room where everything was a pale blue, except one red bowl. To connect myself physically to this idea, I would wear outfits where I only had one red thing on (one red sock, sparkly red glass earrings, a red hair tie, red fingernails) in the midst of an entire pale-yellow ensemble. I became obsessed with red's power to drive everything else it came in contact with. So, imagine my surprise, after the thoughts of such a summer, when I came upon Stein's poem and its line seemingly directed at me, "If red is in everything it is not necessary."

In classes I have taught on color and poetry, I often start with a set of exercises focusing on color within this poem. We read the poem and then I start asking questions steeped in her line: *What does red make you think of? What would happen if red is in everything? What if this room were suddenly all red?* I wear one red piece of clothing or jewelry that day and use it as a visual backdrop to the discussion. The conversation eventually turns to blood, even if it takes a while. I always make sure that it does.

Blood could not be more important to Stein's line and to the exercise. After all, what is the effect of spaces drenched in red, but that they look as if they are covered in blood. I think entirely red rooms look like they are drenched in blood, even if they are just painted. There is an alarm in the color red that seems to indicate that blood has been spilled. A place where red is literally in everything is one where I see there is danger.

In *The Shining*, there is a scene in which Jack Nicholson's murderous and alcoholic character, Jack Torrance, while drunk, first meets the ghost of Delbert Grady (the hotel's past caretaker, who killed his family, including his twin daughters). In this scene, Delbert Grady convinces Jack Nicholson to reenact his own horrible crime, and the bathroom where they are talking is all red. (Although I might add that there are some white tiles in it to lighten the mood.)

Whenever I watch that particular scene, I think of Stein's line, and think: What does it mean again that red is *necessary*? Red has a necessity to express something intense, and when it is everywhere it is not necessary, because then everything is intense. Which is impossible, because intensity is relational. But more on that another time.

Maybe this is like this red bathroom, where an evil ghost meets an evil man, to transfer the metaphysical power of evil. After all, time is a corkscrew, a gyre. Could it be that all beings meet their match in a place of color intensity?

Blood is red. Red is blood. When you see your own blood outside of your body, you know something is wrong (unless it is expected). If red (blood) were everywhere, there would be no need for red and blood, and so forth.

There are not enough books that focus on one color, but one I deeply love is William Gass's 1976 *On Being Blue*, where he bombastically states, "Blue postures, attitudes, blue thoughts, blue gestures . . . is it the form or content that turns blue when these are?"

It is hard to know if it is the word that becomes its color in a poem when a color is used. But what is true is that when a poem uses the right color, when the color becomes a thing, then it makes a space in the mind for the color.

Another great book is *Bluets*, Maggie Nelson's lyrical meditations on the color blue. In her book, she sees blue as an intense, burning color:

> 2. And so I fell in love with a color—in this case, the color blue—as if falling under a spell, a spell I fought to stay under and get out from under, in turns.
>
> 3. Well, and what of it? A voluntary delusion, you might say. That each blue object could be a kind of burning bush, a secret code meant for a single agent, an X on a map too diffuse ever to be unfolded in entirety but that contains the knowable universe. How could all the shreds of blue garbage bags stuck in brambles, or the bright blue tarps flapping over every shanty and fish stand in the world, be, in essence, the fingerprints of God? *I will try to explain this.*

Sometimes I like to imagine red objects as their equal frequency in a blue shade, as painted in the same intensity of their redness as a twin blueness. When switching the color of objects in your imagination, you change everything about them and what surrounds them.

For example, if I were imagining a woman with bright red-orange lips right now (and hey, why not?), I might in my mind then imagine her with lips the color of lapis lazuli cream. If I imagine a love scene with a bright red dress and some red wine, I can then easily see in my mind the same scene, but severely altered with a bright blue dress and navy-colored wine.

Paul Celan's "Death Fugue" sees blue as a color symbolizing evil. Here are just the first two stanzas, translated by Jerome Rothenberg:

Black milk of morning we drink you at dusktime
we drink you at noontime and dawntime we drink you at night
we drink and drink
we scoop out a grave in the sky where it's roomy to lie
There's a man in this house who cultivates snakes and who writes
who writes when it's nightfall *nach Deutschland* your golden hair
 Margareta
he writes it and walks from the house and the stars all start flashing he
 whistles his dogs to draw near
whistles his Jews to appear starts us scooping a grave out of sand
he commands us play up for the dance

Black milk of morning we drink you at night
we drink you at dawntime and noontime we drink you at dusktime
we drink and drink
There's a man in this house who cultivates snakes and who writes

who writes when it's nightfall *nach Deutschland* your golden hair
Margareta
your ashen hair Shulamite we scoop out a grave in the sky where it's
roomy to lie
He calls jab it deep in the soil you lot there you other men sing and play
he tugs at the sword in his belt he swings it his eyes are blue
jab your spades deeper you men you other men play up again for the
dance

Celan's poem reminds us what poetry can do and what brutality it can commemorate. The blue eye of the Nazi symbolizes the idea of an Aryan race. The whole history of the Holocaust is summed up in the choice of this blue eye, not green or brown, and the black milk is the doom of annihilation, of hopelessness. The golden hair of the lucky Margareta and the ashen hair of Shulamite echo with perfect color the disparity between the hunter and the hunted.

A similar perfect choice of color to memorialize brutality is in the closing lines of Sylvia Plath's "Fever 103°":

Does not my heat astound you! And my light!
All by myself I am a huge camellia
Glowing and coming and going, flush on flush.

I think I am going up,
I think I may rise——
The beads of hot metal fly, and I love, I

Am a pure acetylene
Virgin
Attended by roses,

By kisses, by cherubim,
By whatever these pink things mean!
Not you, nor him

Nor him, nor him
(My selves dissolving, old whore petticoats)——
To Paradise.

Maggie Nelson, in *The Art of Cruelty: A Reckoning*, has referred to Plath's choice of pink in "whatever these pink things mean!" as being savagely "sarcastic." Perhaps this is true, as Plath's use of the casual "whatever" when discussing a person rising in hot red and pink colors dying and/or rising up "To Paradise" hurts any sense of sentimentality when you think about it. Of course, these "pink things" are not the simple feminine attributes of the poem's femalish persona. Instead they are more the pinkness of disembodied flesh, skinned and dead as an animal object. These "pink things" that are sort of beside the point. The bodies and flesh we are all housed in.

What these poems do is to turn color on its head. Blue, a calming color, burns with unlivable intensity in Maggie Nelson's blue poems and the steel gaze of the Nazi murderer in Celan's. The sweetness and girlyness of pink, a color to adorn a girl baby's room (for maybe the last one hundred years at least), becomes the soft and unsubstantial, unimportant flesh to house the spirit in Plath's poem.

We are left with the question: What is it that these poems can do with color, and how do they continue to show us what poems can do?

FUTURE USES OF COLOR IN POETRY; OR, THE SOUND OF A POEM IS THE SOUND OF A COLOR, IS THE PROGRESSION OF THE SPECTRUM; AND, THE PROBLEM OF INDIGO

Contemporary American poets have boundaries to cross when using color in their work. David Batchelor famously argued in *Chromophobia* (2000) that since ancient times, Westerners have had a fear of using too much color. Isn't this true today? In the corporate culture that pervades our everyday lives, in the professionalization that pervades all things now in America (or at least it feels this way), we are often warned about being "too colorful."

A recent Google search I did for "power colors," where my intent was to use these colors for spiritual practices, produced a whole host of websites warning job seekers and company employees to avoid wearing "too much color." Why is this? Is it that color distracts one from one's corporate path? Is it that color ignites the spirit, a dormant light? Does the spirit have no place in one's work anymore?

It's not much to think about that we don't already know. If you were to buy a house today on any random street in America and were to decide to paint the outside bright turquoise with neon yellow and orange accents, you might get more than just a few strange looks. More likely you would be branded a weirdo, a crazy person, even someone dangerous. The value of your house would decline with its new colors. Even in its absence, color contains more power than we give it credit for.

Think right now of the last time you read a poem with the perfect color. What color was it? Was it an obvious one? A blue sky, a green tree, a red rose, a yellow sun? Did it symbolize something: a black door, a white dress? How did the expected or unexpected color put spirit in the poem. Was the sun violet? We all need to know about the violet sun. Questions about colors are good questions to ask ourselves.

If we think of the old, tired line "Roses are red," we can see how far colors in poems have taken us already and how far they might go. The line, seemingly simple, contains our potential future of using color in poems. After all, to assert roses are red is a pretty grandiose assertion. How can we know, of course, that the sample rose is not also blue or white or yellow-red or a million colors, too? Now with advances in nanotechnology research, we are learning that colors are not as they appear to be. Though red appears red to us, on a smaller, imperceptible scale, anything red is gold. It is important to think of the almost histrionic assertion of a poet in naming a color, that when a poet says that there is something called red in the first place, they have great arrogance. Because colors themselves are not real, but in poems they are the connection between the real and dream worlds, are reunifications of self with its dreaming self.

If we consider how Stein took us a bit further with her famous "Rose is a rose is a rose is a rose," we can see even more clearly the direction that poems might go. We might ask ourselves: What color is Stein's rose? How might such a line contain the color red (its expectation) and also other colors?

There are so many ways that future poems can use even just the color red. In a 1930 essay from *The Scientific Monthly*, Dr. George R. Stewart explained how modern poetry has the ability to show us not only color, but a "technique of hue," due largely in part to the advancement of science. To illustrate this, he outlined over ten ways red was used in Amy Lowell's work, such as "'crimson butterflies,' . . . 'vermillion fishes,' . . .

'blood-orchid tips of mountains,' 'copper,' 'maroon,' 'ruby,' . . . [and] 'carnation,'" comparing these reds to Chaucer's rudimentary (in Stewart's opinion) use of plain "red," over and over again, without recording the possible variations.

Certainly a rose can be red, but it can also be a rose (containing red), a rose rose, or even a carnation. And red can be many things. Aside from variations in color, there are, just to begin, the multichromatics that now appear in car paint and nail polish for poets to consider. When describing these new colors, a poem can refer to red as red-green or red-silver or also somehow evoke a consistent color shift of red to green to purple to copper to blue, that all occurs within the span of a few seconds.

I like what poetry can do when it is written by people who perceive and process color differently than most of us. In 1970, poet Hannah Weiner fasted for twenty-one days and wrote about how she began to see more clearly the color essence of things in a journal called *The Fast*. In her record, objects, with their necessary color auras, were always more than the color they were. They were also the radiating colors around them.

Future poetry can take its cues for what colors mean to language-makers who aren't poets. In his *Born on a Blue Day* (2007), autistic savant Daniel Tammet describes what colors mean to him:

> Some words are perfect fits for the things they describe. A raspberry is both a red word and a red fruit, while *grass* and *glass* are both green words that describe green things. Words beginning with the letter *T* are always orange like a tulip or a tiger or a tree in autumn, when the leaves turn to orange.
>
> Conversely, some words do not seem to me to fit the things they describe: *geese* is a green word but describes white birds (*heese* would seem a better choice to me), the word *white* is blue while *orange* is clear and

> shiny like ice. *Four* is a blue word but a pointy number, at least to me. The color of *wine* (a blue word) is better described by the French word *vin*, which is purple.

Poetry can learn from people like Tammet and others on the autism spectrum. Although it is not fully understood by researchers, there is the idea that color, with processes like synesthesia, is a sensual thing, that a word might have its own nonobvious color. And that "*geese* is a green word" even when a goose might not be green, and that words have their own objective properties, and are objects, after all.

It has always troubled me that representations of the rainbow contain six colors, but the visible spectrum contains seven. We all remember drawing rainbows as children. Rainbows are made up of red, orange, yellow, green, blue, and purple. But visible light is made up of red, orange, yellow, green, blue, indigo, and violet, the spectrum we know lovingly as ROYGBIV.

I always take for granted that purple and violet are in some way the same color. But what is indigo.

Indigo is a problem. Is the possibility of indigo the possibility of the wild wind. Is it the possibility of the wild wind in the space of the word? Is it a wild animal, a being beyond? Maybe if colors show us what is possible to do in a poem, indigo is the problem of poetry. Because if indigo, a seeming child of blue and violet, is included in the spectrum, then why isn't teal or turquoise (the children of green and blue)? Why isn't fire-orange part of the spectrum, or marigold? Where are these colors?

And if indigo is possible, then maybe this is a reminder of what all poems can do. That all poems are the space between the real and the dream worlds, the platform between the living and the dead.

Indigo is blue like the you of me or you
Ebony is darker than the deepest
Emerald like the water we swam in for a while
To a man of many colors I give word

ALELA DIANE

Again from *Theory of Colours*, Goethe writes:

> If we may at all hope that natural history will gradually be modified by the principle of deducing the ordinary appearances of nature from higher phenomena . . . As colour, in its infinite variety, exhibits itself on the surface of living beings, it becomes an important part of the outward indications, by means of which we can discover what passes underneath.

Certainly color, like sound, is one way to understand the spirit. The poem, with its physical imagination of color, wind, and sound, is another. Perhaps the purpose of a life is not to understand the spirit, and so using colors in a poem, using music to write a poem, is not important then either. But whatever it is we make of it, I say the delight of life will always be the point, the sharp and searing blue-green mystery, the reason to do anything at all, tied up in the bloom of one's spirit, reunified in life, reignited by color. Yes, poetry is an important delight of life.

But what does this mean for poets and poems? The other day was beautiful weather and in the evening I could see the pink and purple of the sunset affect the clouds. As Stevens writes in "A Rabbit as King of the Ghosts":

The difficulty to think at the end of day,
When the shapeless shadow covers the sun
And nothing is left except light on your fur—

Sometimes our words contain at least a handful of colors within them. This is what the poets know. The poet Meghan Maguire Dahn told me recently that the word *livid* means to become dark purpled and blued with anger or red and flushed with anger or white with shock. It comes from the Latin word *livēre*, to be bluish, but this bluishness somehow has transferred over into the colors of the dead—as Mary Shelley wrote, "lips . . . livid with the hue of death."

I once loved a person who loved the color violet so much that I became purple with my love. Beyond a passion of love, infused with blood, I wasn't even red, I became violet. To become him, I sailed past the problems of indigo. Was he, was I. Was he not all forms of flight?

Maybe this is what a poem can do. And perhaps it is true what they say—poetry is a destructive force. To crush all the colors of the spectrum. The pink and purple of the sunset. How is this not one thing?

The first time I fell in love (this was not with the violet one), I got very sick within the first year of our relationship, and my love brought me David Ferry's translation of *Gilgamesh* to read in bed. Between fevers, I only remembered the blue of the poem's lapis lazuli.

Perhaps I will sail across a poem when I sail across the sunset. Whatever it is these pink things mean.

Or maybe it is like, as Nina Simone sang, "I intend to be independently blue." Of course, I do, too.

We create poetry in a multicolored universe. Not a path, but a corkscrew. Not a spectrum, but a gyre. Perhaps the stages of death, containing all forms of flight, are our rainbow.

Whatever it is, it is a truly tangled rainbow.

Until we figure it out, I look to poetry to help me unravel it.

THE BEAST

HOW POETRY MAKES US HUMAN

Don't say that you love me!
Just tell me that you want me!
Tusk! Tusk! Tusk! Tusk!
FLEETWOOD MAC, "Tusk"

THE ANIMAL

This lecture is called "The Beast: How Poetry Makes Us Human," but it used to be called simply "The Animal."

When I called it "The Animal," I was using the word *animal* for a few reasons. The first is because for a long time I have been interested in the idea of the Wild in poetry, and the idea that poetry is an animal somehow through its wild use of language. I've been invested in the notion of a poem being feral (as Lucie Brock-Broido described this term to her students) and how this ferality could make a being partly *not part of itself* and partly *wholly of the self.*

The wild in poetry is what I've always felt poets carry to the making of new language. I probably formed this idea way back in graduate school, when I studied with the poet James Tate. In his workshops, he didn't always talk that much, but at least once per poem, he'd say something. Sometimes he'd say, this poem is wild or this word or image is wild, and that was the greatest compliment of all. I'd be sitting there waiting and hoping each week he'd say that about something I had done, and sometimes he would. Wildness in poetry, I guess you could say, became then a quality of the ideal.

All poets harness a wildness in the *I* of our poems. An *I* in a poem contains so much ego—is so puffed up with its brute strength—that it is willing to shred itself in the space of the poem. Or, that is to say, it feels so strong and confident to be itself that it feels completely free not to be anything at all.

An *I* in a poem is free because it really can be anything, despite the fact that some of us try to make the *I* the poet ourselves. I guess I mean to say when I know something is wild, I want it to be everything. A poem is wild when it is not predetermined. It can be anything it wants to be, and it does, and it does not give itself away at any point. Like a thing that can breed endlessly, it expands without asking. Like when they sing that song "Wild Thing," do they mean you? They do.

Emily Dickinson talks about the wild:

> Wild nights – Wild nights!
> Were I with thee
> Wild nights should be
> Our luxury!
>
> Futile – the winds –
> To a Heart in port –
> Done with the Compass –
> Done with the Chart!

Rowing in Eden –
Ah – the Sea!
Might I but moor – tonight –
In thee!

This poem at its face seems to be all about love. After all, what is wild love on a wild night? So many songs have been sung about it, and we have loved these songs. I have loved them, at least. Haven't you? But I am not sure that I have ever felt it: this wild love in a wild night, with a wild heart.

Well, certainly I've felt that: a wild heart. I know that I have felt wild sexual passion at least for a moment or two in this lifetime. I know that I have felt wild emotional obsession that I let overtake me to, for example, let me fly across the country for the sake of even just a whiff of it. Sometimes not even for that. Just more for the idea of two people running toward each other in the rain. Like that ever happens. (Will it?)

But I am not sure I have ever known what it is to be in the moon of a wild night. To be wholly engulfed by an animal nature and to have that be in essence about another person, with a spirit, trapped within what is a body, with what we might call a human body full of flames.

I started this lecture with lines from the song "Tusk" from the great band Fleetwood Mac. I have always loved these lines because to me they mean what might be a wild passion, or might seem to be. After all, as the band sings, we want to say to those we love: Don't tell me that you love me, tell me that you want me. The people I have loved the most have always understood me when I have said to them with this song playing in the background: this is the truth about love. What does love care about love? Love is all about what it means to need.

To need to do is at least in part what it means to make you want to do anything. Now that's wild.

I hope that part of what this lecture will make you think about is the question: How does poetry make us human, connect us to what the animal is, and give us guidance to be of and not of the animal? I think poetry does help us do this. One way it does it is to give us a way to relate to animals.

But why are animals important to poetry, you might be asking? Because they are the living travelers with us who are both most like, and unlike, us.

Another way to think about it is that animals are important to us and to poetry because they give us a way to relate to one another. The living us and the dead us and the yet-to-be-born us. The animals within us who can speak our language—the sounds in the letters we have decreed have meaning. Animals connect us to the who-to-be who are waiting to write and rewrite the languages that are yet to be, and they do.

In *The Animal That Therefore I Am*, Jacques Derrida talks about a kind of shame he has felt at the idea of a cat seeing him naked. He describes a sort of *malaise* that the cat might see him as a thing, that he might be seen through the eyes of another—in this case, an animal, a cat—as the animal he really is. He writes:

> Ashamed of what and naked before whom? Why let oneself be overcome with shame? And why this shame that blushes for being ashamed? Especially, I should make clear, if the cat observes me *frontally* naked, face to face, and if I am naked faced with the cat's eyes looking at me from head to toe, as it were just *to see*, not hesitating to concentrate its vision—in order to see, with a view to seeing—in the direction of my sex. *To see*,

> without going to see, without touching yet, and without biting, although that threat remains on its lips or on the tip of the tongue. . . .
>
> Ashamed of what and before whom? Ashamed of being as naked as a beast. It is generally thought . . . that the property unique to animals, what in the last instance distinguishes them from man, is their being naked without knowing it. Not being naked therefore, not having knowledge of their nudity, in short, without consciousness of good and evil.
>
> . . . naked without knowing it, animals would not be, in truth, naked.

I often wonder what insight Derrida gives us with these ideas. And what that means for poetry. If an animal is not conscious of being naked, because being naked is somehow like being wild and being a wild animal, then what does it mean to not care that an animal sees you. Are you then wild, too? Can a poem ever be naked and care or not care if you see it that way? Maybe. Maybe the best poems care about their nakedness, and then they don't.

And if a poem lets itself be shred and does not care that it is naked, then what does that mean about the reader and what the *I* feels for the reader? After all, to let your poem be naked, despite the fact that you know people will read it is, I think, to have the ultimate empathy, the ultimate and absolute trust. To acknowledge that your reader can bite you, but that you are in a dance of the animals. And to acknowledge that a need to express what is our greatest gift as a humanity—the dance of the spirit through the imagination as manifest in language and color—is a need, a want, that you are willing to go into the wild night to achieve. To not say that you love something, to say not just that you love it, but that you want it. Tusk.

As I mentioned above, for a long time, this lecture was titled simply "The Animal." To me, the idea of the wild has always been summed up best by Animal from the Muppets.

No, this is not a joke. I'm not trying to be funny. For many years, my worst fear was an image of Animal, suspended in blankness, looking back at me.

This fear first started when I was very little and had a View-Master with a Muppets reel. The slides started off pleasant enough, with the Muppets in many great locales, a slide or two of Miss Piggy and Kermit in love, and then Rowlf playing the piano. Toward the end, at the penultimate slide, there was Sweetums, all alone against a red background.

If you know the Muppets, you know that Sweetums is a nice muppet, just kind of freaky looking. But he sort of set the stage for what was the last slide of the reel: Animal in a black background, suspended in the universe, a wild thing among the sublime.

Even as an adult, I continued to have this fear. In my midtwenties, I lived in fear that friends who knew I felt this way would somehow find it silly enough to scare me. I used to make one of my best friends promise me he wouldn't sneakily put this picture on my desktop when he borrowed my computer, as he was extremely fond of pranks. He never did, thankfully. But I often watched who I told. Have you ever noticed how people can be very mean when you tell them your fears? They sometimes lie in wait to snap them back at you.

At age twenty-seven, I started a master's program at Harvard, and they had the requisite beginning of the program celebration at the big science museum in Boston. I went with my then-boyfriend to the party and we looked around at all of this amazing stuff in the museum and then we saw some View-Masters, and without thinking I picked one up and lo and behold the first image was of all of the Muppets in a '70s golden background. I shrieked, and my boyfriend came running to my side. He looked and flipped to the next image and there it was—he laughed—there was Animal, one slide away from my view. Even in my moment of glory, there was Animal waiting in his vortex, sitting there, ready to look at me.

As we can see, because I am having this discussion with you, I am not scared of Animal like I once was. When my husband, Thom, and I first moved in together, I decided maybe I should do some systematic desensitization to get rid of my fear. I wrote about Animal on an old blog, which is still online, as a way of getting past my phobia. I wrote that Frank Oz developed him in conjunction with images of Mick Fleetwood playing the drums. Have you ever watched a video of Mick Fleetwood playing live? It makes sense, although I feel nothing at all for Mick Fleetwood. Don't say that you love me, tell me that you want me. Tusk.

After all of this, my fear subsided. It is almost gone now, but even so, you won't ever catch me looking at too many pictures of Animal before bed.

What was I always so scared of? Why did the image scare me? It is of course the gaze back at me, in the View-Master, with no way to escape the gaze. It is the intense gaze of passion I had always wanted and feared. Animal, in his puppet eyes, needed me in that black space. Just like my reader needs me.

Maybe it is that Animal frightened me because he stood for death. That to feel the shred of annihilation is to be a bright-red beast in the midst of the black life. That the ego is shredded again and again. I don't really believe in the afterlife, but I do believe that we come back as spiritual beings into this world again and again, and maybe Animal's eyes said to me, *You know that I know. That I know you.* And maybe I felt a great overwhelming passion for him, because I know, too.

In *The Open: Man and Animal*, Giorgio Agamben writes of the idea of the *Homo sapiens* (which we know means, in Latin, the "wise man") that is, as he puts it, "neither a clearly defined species nor a substance; it is, rather, a machine or device for producing the recognition of the human." He goes on:

> In medieval iconography, the ape holds a mirror in which the man who sins must recognize himself as *simia dei* [ape of God]. In Linnaeus's optical machine, whoever refuses to recognize himself in the ape, becomes one: to paraphrase Pascal, *qui fait l'homme, fait le singe* [he who acts the man, acts the ape]. This is why at the end of the introduction to the *Systema*, Linnaeus, who defined *Homo* as the animal that is only if it recognizes that it *is not*, must put up with apes disguised as critics climbing on his shoulders to mock him: . . . [that is why I endured the derisive laughter of snarling satyrs and the exultation of monkeys leaping onto my shoulders].

Agamben wants us to realize that to not recognize the animal in us is to not recognize our own divinity. For if we do not realize we are animal, then we cannot be human. To not see ourselves gaze upon what we see in the animals of us is to always be the animal, to not let the wild overtake us like an ocean, but to fear the wild and all that it is capable of doing to us.

Maybe Animal is the poem I have not yet written (and maybe never will), and this is why I fear him.

In "Che cos'è la poesia?" ("What sort of thing is poetry?" written in response to that question for an Italian journal), Jacques Derrida says that a poem is sort of like a hedgehog thrown out into the middle of a road:

> Rolled up in a ball, prickly with spines, vulnerable and dangerous, calculating and ill-adapted (because it makes itself into a ball, sensing the danger on the autoroute, it exposes itself to an accident). No poem without accident, no poem that does not open itself like a wound, but no poem that is not also just as wounding.

Maybe if the gaze of the wild is the poem that you want to, but can never, write, then in Derrida's definition, the poem is the thing that you run over on the road that is willing to get hit, to open itself up to accident. That which is animal—in this case, a hedgehog—both allows itself to be wounded and also, if necessary, to do the wounding.

Earlier in this book, in "Poetry, Ghosts, and the Shared Imagination," I talk about the imagination as the space that a poem can open up where we can commune as humans and even as human ghosts. Where the living and dead can gaze upon each other. It all invites further questions: What is a ghost, and what is consciousness after we die? And then following whatever the answer is, we might ask, too: What is an animal, and what is animal consciousness? Will we ever know?

Some people say that they infantilize the things that they love, they go *goo goo gaga* and all that. But I've thought that poets often animalize the things they love, and maybe to make the things and people real in poems is to make them animals in poems. And maybe to make a thing an animal in a poem is to make it, once and for all, real.

LUCY

What is so real as the cry of a child?
A rabbit's cry may be wilder
But it has no soul.

SYLVIA PLATH, "Kindness"

For about a year, I prepared an animal altar in my living room because I knew I was facing the end of the road with the only dog I had ever had, Lucinda Labchow Lasky, or Lucy, as I called her.

My dog Lucy died six summers ago when she was seventeen and a half years old. I got her when she was around two, and like most dog owners, I will never forget the day that I met her.

I had always wanted a dog growing up, and I promised myself that at age twenty, I would get one. And I did.

I went to a pound one day near my apartment in St. Louis and started looking at a reddish chow. (I love chows because of their fur, and I love fur.) And as I was looking at this other dog, a male, I heard a whimper and felt something at my back and looked behind me and Lucy, a black chow mix, had her paw out to me, was actually pawing at me, and she was saying to me with her gaze, "Get me out of this place. I'm yours. You're mine."

Lucy was very healthy through our life together, but one winter she came down with a very bad form of bladder cancer that spread and eventually killed her. When she died, I put her ashes on the animal altar I had been preparing for them, and that is where they sit now, in a rather ugly green-and-white floral metal urn.

During the nine months that Lucy was dying, I really struggled a lot but also came to terms with her death. Going through this extreme grief and dealing with it while she was still alive was and continues to be something that is hard to explain. A lot of people just roll their eyes and say, oh that's a dog, that's just an animal, please just get it together. It's not a child. If you had had a child then, you would have understood why she wasn't like a child. But the people who understood and continue to understand what she meant to me and were there for me during those months are the people who right now, at this point, I continue to love the most as humans.

During the months that she was dying, I used to leave her in the apartment to go teach or go somewhere, and sometimes I'd be almost all the way down the three flights of stairs of our apartment building and I'd rush back—I'd run back, breathlessly—and bust open the door and scream, "Lucy, I love you," and run to her and hug her and shower her with kisses.

It seems so dramatic as I tell you this now. And I know it was kind of dramatic to her then. I swear she'd kind of roll her eyes when she'd see me running back, wild-eyed. But we were old friends. She was used to me and my dramas. She let me hug her. What choice did she have. We belonged to each other.

In his book *Dog Years: A Memoir*, Mark Doty writes that after he put his dog, Arden, to sleep, and laid his body in the back of the vet's truck, he arranged "his head and neck so he look[ed] more comfortable, even though," as he writes, he knew it was "absurd." This is the sort of thing we do for any animal we must say goodbye to. We treat them as we might want others to treat us.

Maybe what I felt for Lucy is what they explain it is to love madly. I loved her without question. I loved the beast of her in me wildly. I loved the beast in me, madly, which I was, when we were together as two animals. She knew I was a poet and I knew her life was poetry, too. And we were a poem and we will always be. And in the poems of her and in these words now, I feel she is still alive.

WHAT IS A BEAST TO US: ANNE SEXTON, THE RAT, AND THE SNAKE

Anne Sexton's posthumously published book *45 Mercy Street* has a section of eighteen poems about animals called "Bestiary U.S.A." Each focuses on a particular animal: a bat, a hog, a porcupine, a hornet, a star-nosed mole, a snail, a lobster, a snake, a moose, a sheep, a cockroach, a raccoon, a seal, an earthworm, a whale, a horse, a june bug, and a gull. Sexton studies and describes each animal to seek out its spirit, to uncover what makes it wild and human, in order to empower the reader to take on its strength—to ultimately use each as a cathartic symbol. In each poem, Sexton, as in all of her work, is willing to let her lyric go wild, for the sake of this catharsis and empowerment.

Later in the same book is the following poem, "Cigarettes and Whiskey and Wild, Wild Women":

> Perhaps I was born kneeling,
> born coughing on the long winter,
> born expecting the kiss of mercy,
> born with a passion for quickness
> and yet, as things progressed,
> I learned early about the stockade
> or taken out, the fume of the enema.
> By two or three I learned not to kneel,

not to expect, to plant my fires underground
where none but the dolls, perfect and awful,
could be whispered to or laid down to die.

Now that I have written many words,
and let out so many loves, for so many,
and been altogether what I always was—
a woman of excess, of zeal and greed,
I find the effort useless.
Do I not look in the mirror,
these days,
and see a drunken rat avert her eyes?
Do I not feel the hunger so acutely
that I would rather die than look
into its face?
I kneel once more,
in case mercy should come
in the nick of time.

What I have always loved about this poem is how, by the end of it, Sexton has turned herself, her persona, into a rat. She sees herself, her own shame for her drunkenness, for her failure of being a human, as a kind of turning into an animal, an extreme empathy through animalization. It is through the mirror that she is able to be both the gazer and the thing being gazed upon, animal and human in communion. It is through the face of an animal—a rat in this case, one of our most hated animals—it is through seeing herself in the face of the rat that she begs the reader for the mercy that most likely will never come. After all, who could feel mercy for a rat, our mortal enemy? Perhaps if you read this poem in all good faith, you could.

Lots of poets see a poem as a place to demonstrate the interaction between their persona and the animal and to become one with the animal. This is a way that poetry can teach us to be human.

For example, Emily Dickinson writes of almost stepping on a snake:

> A narrow Fellow in the Grass
> Occasionally rides –
> You may have met him? Did you not
> His notice instant is –

The Grass divides as with a Comb –
A spotted Shaft is seen,
And then it closes at your Feet
And opens further on –

He likes a Boggy Acre –
A Floor too cool for Corn –
But when a Boy and Barefoot
I more than once at Noon

Have passed I thought a Whip Lash
Unbraiding in the Sun
When stooping to secure it
It wrinkled And was gone –

Several of Nature's People
I know, and they know me
I feel for them a transport
Of Cordiality

But never met this Fellow
Attended or alone
Without a tighter Breathing
And Zero at the Bone.

Here, Dickinson writes of the pain of possibly stepping on a snake, the anticipation of "Unbraiding in the Sun," the horrible pain and possibility of pain of being bit. To fear what might happen to the body from the action of the animal. She ends the poem with the idea that the sight of the snake produces tight breath and the "Zero at the Bone." The nadir point of all fear, to be zero at the bone and to fear the bite that goes into the bone, past the point of superficial pain, to the point of pain where most pain dares not to go. The pain where there will be no more place to go in this body.

That the snake brings a person to the height of fear, at the core of what fear could be, is what is amazing about the snake and poems about snakes. Is this because a human is fearful when it sees a snake, because a snake represents death? Or is it too because the ego seeks to be overtaken, to become one with the animal, in this case a hated animal, a snake?

Gordon Grice, in *The Book of Deadly Animals*, writes of a strange encounter with a snake and of complete human and animal conflation:

> One morning in 2001, an American herpetologist was on a scientific expedition to Myanmar when, in a careless moment, he allowed a krait collected by his party to bite his finger. He briefed his followers on what to expect. He would, he said, be conscious through the entire forty-eight hours it would take for his body to process the toxin, though he would soon be unable to speak. His colleagues watched him carefully. Before long, he couldn't open his eyes except with his fingers. His breath began to labor. As predicted, he lost the power of speech and could communicate with his colleagues only by writing notes. In the afternoon his friends kept him alive by blowing air into his lungs. "Blow harder," he advised them in a note. They tried. But a few moments later he changed his mind. "Let me di," he wrote, and reluctantly they did.

The thing that has always struck me about Grice's description of this event is: What is and what was this "careless moment"? What did it mean for a herpetologist to have a careless moment with a poisonous snake, in which he knew exactly what it would do to him—that it would kill him? Was he truly careless, and did he forget what would happen to him with the bite? Did he in that moment desire to become one with the animal? Certainly we are not meant to see the snake at fault through his bite, the way we might if it had snuck up on him. The snake was simply doing what it was meant to do and the scientist, too, seemed in this "careless" moment to be doing the inevitable. A strange fate where animal and human are together through dying.

The other curious part of the encounter was the poem he wrote in his note. He wrote in fractured language, "Let me di." The -e an afterthought he couldn't bring himself to have the desire anymore to bring out of himself.

This poem, "Let me di," makes me think of a poem by William Carlos Williams, "The Last Words of My English Grandmother":

> There were some dirty plates
> and a glass of milk
> beside her on a small table
> near the rank, disheveled bed—
>
> Wrinkled and nearly blind
> she lay and snored
> rousing with anger in her tones
> to cry for food,
>
> Gimme something to eat—
> They're starving me—
> I'm all right—I won't go
> to the hospital. No, no, no
>
> Give me something to eat!
> Let me take you

to the hospital, I said
and after you are well

you can do as you please.
She smiled, Yes
you do what you please first
then I can do what I please—

Oh, oh, oh! she cried
as the ambulance men lifted
her to the stretcher—
Is this what you call

making me comfortable?
By now her mind was clear—
Oh you think you're smart
you young people,

she said, but I'll tell you
you don't know anything.
Then we started.
On the way

we passed a long row
of elms. She looked at them
awhile out of
the ambulance window and said,

What are all those
fuzzy-looking things out there?
Trees? Well, I'm tired
of them and rolled her head away.

When the herpetologist let the snake bite him, did he do it to become one with the animal? Is this what it means, as Plath wrote in her poem about her horse, Ariel, to be:

> Suicidal, at one with the drive
> Into the red
>
> Eye, the cauldron of morning.

When the grandmother in Williams's poem didn't care anymore about the trees—their name, their shape—because she was tired of the distinctions of life and wanted to die, did she become one with her own sense of the animal?

Here I can't help but think of Bhanu Kapil's *Humanimal: A Project for Future Children*, in which she reimagines the plight of the famous "Bengali wolf girls," Kamala and Amala, who were found running through the wild in 1921 and were taken back into Indian society. In the book, she attempts to give them voice through language and imagines what it was like to be a wolf girl and then forced to be just a girl. After all, something was lost. I think too of the story of Romulus and Remus, raised by their wolf mother, with this animal upbringing a perfect preparation to set them up to begin (arguably) the most important city of all time.

To let the animal overpower us is to let the poem overpower us. A poem has an overpowering love.

THE WILD MIND AND THE FOREST

There is a famous story of how when Allen Ginsberg was doing meditation, he often carried around a notebook in which to write his lines of poetry. One day during meditation, the leader of the group said, "Put that away, let the lines go." When Ginsberg protested, "But I will lose my lines," the man replied, "Trust your mind."

What does it mean for a poet to trust their mind? There is the overpowering love of a poem, the overpowering love of the mind, of poetry. Poetry is not precious. It is a gentle and awful animal. One that you can trust will come back again and again.

One time a few years ago, I was having a conversation with Elizabeth Metzger. She was once my student and is now one of my best friends. She is a spectacular poet and wrote a book called *The Spirit Papers*. When we were in our workshop together more than five years ago, she was trying to figure out how to harness the place in herself where poems come from, to begin anew, to be a New Elizabeth, as she called it.

One day I tried to tell her that in all of us are two beings: an unconscious and a conscious one. They are like an id/animal and an ego/human, but also not. But in the space of writing a poem, they must be in concert. They are like a mouse and a human within a kitchen—in a strange harmony of nature, of nonprecious natural order. If they see each other in the kitchen, they will not like it. But there is a way (sadly for all of us who hate rodents) that they can coexist. They must pass and try not to look upon each other too long. They cannot get caught in the View-Master together. There must be a place for both to escape.

It is crushing to be one with the wild. But in poetry it is important, and however a poet figures out how to do so is an important thing to understand and uncover. The ego and id are friends with a person, and they are not animals. But animals, poems, ids, and egos are all part of human consciousness. Still, I always ask myself, what is human? Or, what is a poem? Now I ask, what is an animal? Is it the wild knocking in the other room at night? I cannot look upon it for fear it might overcome me.

I was not with Lucy on the day she died—I was in Paris, doing something, which seemed so unimportant both then and now. On the final day, the cancer caused her blood to turn upon itself. My husband said that even when Lucy was in the worst of her pain, as she began to bleed out in the car on the way to the vet where he took her to die, she did not bite him. But held her teeth out, as if to say, I could, but I won't.

I have always thought that to be a poet you have to deal with your own death. Maybe this is dealing with the animal inside of you. You have to know that your words will die and that people will read them. That they will see you and your words dead and that they will hold you in that kind of intimacy. And that you eat and have sex and breathe and poop all for a bunch of words that will die the second you put them down, just sit like a bunch of flattened nothings that somehow you give as a gift to all of us. To care again that the fuzzy shapes out there are called trees.

Wallace Stevens's poem "Poetry Is a Destructive Force" reminds us of what both a wild animal and a poem are. He writes:

> That's what misery is,
> Nothing to have at heart.
> It is to have or nothing.
>
> It is a thing to have,
> A lion, an ox in his breast,
> To feel it breathing there.

Corazon, stout dog,
Young ox, bow-legged bear,
He tastes its blood, not spit.

He is like a man
In the body of a violent beast.
Its muscles are his own . . .

The lion sleeps in the sun.
Its nose on its paws.
It can kill a man.

How is the poem, poetry itself, this destructive force? How is it like the lion sleeping in the sun with its nose on its paws? It can kill a man, but it doesn't (yet). It bides its time. Is it the reader of the poem or the writer of the poem who is most in danger of death? Certainly it is both.

When I was nineteen, I visited a friend in Pennsylvania, and we took a trip to the Poconos and stayed in a little family house in the woods. I used to run a lot, it was a compulsion then to run at least two hours a day, and I ran through the woods one day, a teenager from the non-wild suburbs, with no fear of what animals I might encounter. For much of the time, I only noticed the large and overpowering trees.

As I ran and ran, a giant stag burst in on my path. In my memory, as it ran through the trees and past me, its antlers were the size of a house. It was likely over 300 pounds. It never occurred to me then that it could have killed me. And it only maybe occurs to me now. It ran so fast that it was an illusion. The way it broke in, quietly, and then it was gone. It never made a sound. There is no sound in my memory. Is this like what ghosts are? Are beastly ghosts an illusion, too? Is it true that the deer and the dachshund really are one?

Or maybe this deer came into my life in that moment to be my ars poetica.

Out of a clearing the poem comes from your everyday life. It surprises you. It comes in and then it is gone. Like an amethyst can be a purple wonderland from inside the rock, so too can the deer emerge from the forest and then go back into it again. So too can a poem burst out and then go away. It has its own force. And so be it.

THERE, THERE

Now that she's gone, I wonder: What did Lucy teach me about living? I think she taught me: The world is a dirge. Ultimately all you love is a death song.

What does poetry teach us? That the death song can be beautiful. That you can lose and lose again, but that people will listen to you. And that poems are the electrical outlet into a humanity that has found a song to cope with its death.

It's true, then. To cope is to never die, too.

What does the animal do? It reminds us that living and dying is the thing we must do. Its simplicity is the poetry of living.

Or like what Stein said. I am I because my little dog knows me.

As Stein wrote in her poem "A Dog":

> A little monkey goes like a donkey that means to say that means to say that more sighs last goes. Leave with it. A little monkey goes like a donkey.

I was because my dog knew me. What is the poet but the wild unknown?

What did my dog teach me about being human? To be gentle. To be gentle and wild and to be able to, but not to, bite everyone.

What does poetry teach us about being human? Maybe what Charles Baudelaire said, that "remembering is only a new form of suffering."

Or maybe that "poetry is a destructive force."

And maybe it is true what Stevens said. The look of all of my animals in the rain. That is the thing I will always remember. To be an animal in the rain. But to be gentle. To care. To look into the living eye and see itself. The red eye, the cauldron of morning. But also the blue one, too. The violet eye in the wild night. That is the self. That is the self worth speaking. That is the work we do, as poets, as humans.

Is it possible to ever meet a beast who has never seen the snow? If it is, try to be gentle, as you both pass along on your way.

Be careful, too, when handling the snakes. They, like all of us, do what they must do.

So: When you meet the animal in the dead of night, make sure that it doesn't notice you.

That's all.

THE BEES

BEES AS THE GHOST: AN INTRODUCTION

I have come to speak to you about the bees—the bees and poetry—and the strange hexacomb, which governs everything.

I owe a lot of my thinking about bees and their mystical power to a movie I saw with my husband, Thom Donovan, now over ten years ago, on one of our first dates. I was living in Philadelphia and would visit him in his apartment in the Lower East Side in Manhattan, and one night we watched a movie, *Wax, or the Discovery of Television Among the Bees*.

I remember how fond he was of the movie, how he seemed to be enraptured by the strange narrative of it.

In the movie, a man, who is the main narrator, realizes that for his job, he is actually making missiles for the first Iraq war in the 1990s. He has a breakdown of sorts, realizing that he is actually doing harm, that his work is, in part, that of a mass murderer.

After having this realization, he turns to his work with the bees, as he is also a bee husbander. He seems to start to have a telepathic communication with the bees and to communicate with the bees as with his dead ancestors.

The movie becomes, then, a mystical conversion between self and other, for every time he is with the bees, he has visions of his ancestors and sees the connections across time. Especially because his ancestors are Iraqi, and so the missiles he has created are being used to kill his past and future selves.

When I first saw the movie, it did not make sense exactly. But even though the movie itself was strange—there is something about bees, buzzing and humming on a television set, that does make sense.

As a poet, I have often seen the imagination as a kind of television set with the hum of the dead. Isn't speaking to the dead what poets do? Aren't poems a conversion, a mystical conversion between self and other?

In life, I often think of my own body as a kind of conduit and I look at things in the everyday—a car here, the plants, maybe a road—and I imagine these things, these objects, my spirit in another body, in another time. I hum in and out and what does anything make of me. I know, for sure, that I have been here before. I have walked this earth before as a being, as a person, and I have spoken to come back, and speak again.

Whatever the case, as poet, in poetry, things that do not involve the occult—frankly, they just bore me. Bees are the hidden.

I wrote this lecture for the bees, and what, as a living ghost, they have done for me.

THE BEES AS THE THINGS THAT WE HAVE DONE

Rudolf Steiner, in his famous lectures on bees, explains how the mystery of the bees is not just that they make honey, but that they create the hexagonal structures that store the food. They are not just creators. They create everything, as everything is self-contained. He writes:

> Having transformed the food by means of its own bodily substances into wax—this the bee produces out of itself—the bees now make a special little container in which to deposit its egg or in which to store up food supplies. This special little vessel is, I should like to say, a really great marvel, It appears to be hexagonal when we look at it from above; looked at from the side it is closed in this way. Eggs can be deposited there, or food can be stored. Each vessel lies next to another; they fit extremely well together, so that this "surface" by which one cell, (for so it is called), is joined to another in the honey-comb, is exceedingly well made use of—the space is well used.

Isn't that the way we always describe a poem? As Williams writes:

> There's nothing sentimental about a machine, and: A poem is a small (or large) machine made of words. When I say there's nothing sentimental about a poem, I mean that there can be no part, as in any other machine, that is redundant.

How isn't what the bee makes, a set of containers of well-used space, like the nonsentimental machine of a poem? Or is the bee's body itself the machine, the honey *and* the wax storage structures the poem, all together, as one thing?

Bees always make me think of telepathy—I think because I have long been in love with the movie *Candyman.*

In that movie, if you haven't seen it, a graduate student named Helen Lyle is conducting an anthropologic study on urban legends and goes to the Chicago housing project Cabrini-Green to study the legend of Candyman.

The story goes that Candyman is a spirit who haunts the project, causing evil and murder, especially when you call for him, and that in real life he was an artist and the son of a slave. He had lived a peaceful life as a successful artist until he fell in love with a white woman and got her pregnant. A lynch mob cut off his painting hand and spread honey on him, and the bees from an apiary stung him to death.

According to legend, when you want to summon Candyman, you turn the lights off, stare into a mirror, and call *Candyman Candyman Candyman Candyman Candyman*, and then he appears. He appears as the summoning of the self in the mirror.

Because he died by bees, he carries a swarm of bees with him. And indeed when he shows up, bees empty out of his cloak, flying everywhere. The image when it happens provides a hum. There is also a sweetness to him, despite his monstrosity, maybe from carrying around throughout time the honey and the bees.

Early on in the movie, after he is summoned, Candyman wants to prove to Helen that he is real and not a story. She wakes from unconsciousness in a woman's apartment, with the woman's baby missing and her dog decapitated, and Helen must defend herself from the frantic mother's attack. After this moment, Helen enters into a love descent with Candyman himself and eventually becomes an otherworldly being with him.

The apartment scene that begins this turn is the most horrific one in the movie. The apartment light is cold, bright—a cheap fluorescence—and the blood everywhere is not softened. As viewers, we know Helen is not to blame, exactly, yet there is guilt nonetheless. After all, we are all here as viewers, implicated in the not-notreal legend—a swarm of bees humming around the story.

And even though the bees stung Candyman to death and are the symbol of destruction, of the demonization of him and Helen and others, the harbingers of death—one can't help but think within the movie that they bring a structure or goodness to the story. They make Candyman real—they are real bees—and carry the dead Candyman upon summoning him. They live and create the neat hexagonal structures of their honeycomb, which is akin to the neat structure of the projects. They hum across a land of spirits that is and is not the real, but they are.

Eric Baus—one of my dearest friends, the kind of inspirational friend that, as Ted Berrigan writes, was that painter I could not get away from—ended his 2009 book *Tuned Droves* with a poem called "Orange Water" that manifests real bees:

> The bloom. The boiling water. Bees. Real flowers release bees. Real flowers bloom orange. Real bees bloom in boiling water. Real water releases bees. Boiling real bees releases flowers. The flowers bloom. The bees bloom. The water blooms. The boiling blooms. Real flowers. Real bees. Real water. Flowers are not real. Bees are not real. Water is not real. Release the bees. Boil the bees. Water the bees. Real water. Orange flowers. Orange water.

This poem has always stuck with me. It seems simple enough—it describes a person (presumably) boiling water in order to separate a solid into its components, to separate liquids—at first the moment really does seem to be about making tea. Even though "Bees" is the third phrase, we still have "Real flowers release bees" and "Real flowers bloom[ing] orange," which all seem real enough. It is not until the "Real water releases bees" that we realize we are in the space of magic. Real water doesn't release bees when it boils. All of sudden nothing is as it seems.

There are "Real flowers. Real bees. Real water," and just as soon the poem tells us none of these things are real. Flowers are not real. Bees are not real. Wait, no! And then, no, even WATER is not real. Water isn't real? But we are made of water. How can this be?

And then the only thing left to do is to release the bees, to boil them, to kill them, water them, soak them in water until they all drown and make us orange flowers and then orange water. That is what a poem can do—it can turn and twist as we boil the water to soak the bees, no, drown and kill the bees, whose death has bloomed the miraculous orange flower, which leads the way.

One January several years ago, I went to Cabrini-Green to see the housing projects in *Candyman*, to see if in real life it was the same as in my memory of its movie depiction. A gorgeous artist and curator, Hamza Walker, took me there in his car. It was snowing badly that night in Chicago. And as we got to the projects, I got out of the car and slid everywhere. I had worn slippery shoes coated in cheap glitter, and the ice and night were slippery, and I fell almost to the ground, but Hamza held me up, told me I needed "some Chicago shoes." The projects had been recently demolished. There was nothing there that was like the movie, like in my memory. We got back in the car, and after looking for a few moments at an empty, snowy field encased in a metal fence, we sped away.

The Roman poet Horace (65–8 BC), in his poem "To Iullus Antonius," famously compares his work as a poet to that of a bee:

. . . Antonius, I

Am like the humble bee, painstakingly
Seeking to find the honey in the thyme
That grows in lowly fragrant groves and grows

Along the watery banks of Tivoli's stream;
My songs are made laboriously and slow.

In this poem, the bee, like the poet, labors, gathering pollen (like language, like memories) so as to make the honey. To make this honey and reconfigure its body processes into wax, to make the comb. And for what? For what we do not know. We only know it is all the plight of both poet and bee.

In the poem, Horace tells Iullus Antonius that this poet's lesser, worldly plight is to celebrate Caesar, whereas Horace's work as a poet is to exalt the immortal, human sun:

"O sun
Alluring and admirable"

During the time Horace wrote, this poet, Iullus Antonius, might have thought that Horace's bee-like work, worshipping the "alluring" sun, was inconsequential compared to the poetic effort he put in to worship the all-powerful Caesar. But we know that Horace's *I* actually does the work of a seer and has an otherworldly master, and that his *I* is one who steadily worships the divine in the natural world and has the ultimate power to conquer the universe.

In Finnish folklore, there is the story of Lemminkäinen, who went to the North Country to try and win the hand of the fairest maiden in the land. An old cowherd, offended by Lemminkäinen's plight, killed him, cut his body into eight pieces, and threw them in the river. Lemminkäinen's mother fished his body pieces out with a magic rake and put the pieces back together again, only to make a speechless doll of a man.

Knowing that she needed to give her son voice again, she called on the bees to help and bring him honey.

But with all that we know of how hard bees work, her bees *really* had to work hard. For Lemminkäinen's sad mother, they traveled to Metsola's fair meadows to get Lemminkäinen a special honey, but this honey did not help him speak. So the bees traveled again, this time across nine lakes to an island, to bring back an even more special and powerful honey. Still even this honey did not help her son.

So, on a third journey, the bees went past the stars to Jumala the Creator's realm and brought back a honey that cured Lemminkäinen, who spoke and was alive again.

The bee holds the magic—honey—that makes the voice of a poet. That can make an *I* speak. And for this reason, the *I* in poems not only becomes the powerful bee, it respects the work ethic of the bee and in many cases tries to emulate it. The *I* becomes humble at the magic of the bee and then takes this magic into their poems.

There are so many bees in poems when you start looking for them. And I have found that once you start looking you can't stop. They almost start to swarm at you.

PLATH AND THE BEES

I don't owe just the movie *Television Among the Bees* to my husband, Thom. I also owe to him the idea of intense autobiography. The drama of which, I owe to the bees.

One time several years ago, I saw Thom give a talk in Bushwick, Brooklyn. I think it was in Bushwick. I remember we were living in

Woodside, Queens, and it was hard to get there, so that's where it must have been.

It was in a small art space that my friend Stacy—a friend of an old friend of a friend, Katie Geha—had organized. I remember that Bernadette Mayer's son was in the audience and I got very nervous to see him. It was like seeing royalty—he was the son of the queen.

I remember I got very, very nervous when Thom introduced the idea of intense autobiography with a discussion of Hannah Weiner, Bernadette Mayer, and then he threw my name in, all weighted, not really discussing my work, but throwing my real name in, as part of this history. And I didn't want to look at anyone as he did this. I felt a real sense of shame.

It made me almost start sweating, and I could tell he was nervous, too, because we assumed people knew we were married so thought this was some sort of trick. Like when people mention their friends in their writing, as I am doing here. We were part of the same hive.

Especially in the first years we were together, I think that Thom wanted to distance his work from mine. I felt ashamed and narcissistic in my shame. Like going to the pool or letting someone see my real face. There was a nakedness to my real name, my real identity. The poet can hide, can hide away, in the space of being a bee, of being a being in the poem, of being just a name.

But this assumption as he spoke my name that day just had so much narcissism. It is hard to know if people even knew we were together, knew what it meant for him to say my name. Out loud. In the public arena.

In his discussion of intense autobiography, he talked about what it meant to use the self as a kind of biopolitic, a kind of body-performance space, what it meant for a female poet to use the events of her life for her art. I think I agree that this is what a bee does, too.

In *Ariel*, Sylvia Plath summons many bees. She uses bees as a kind of battle cry.

In "The Arrival of the Bee Box," she describes the confinement of being a bee, of being a poet, a thing being been, in this lifetime, in a box that by the end of the poem is only "temporary."

And her desire is to give these little bees, these poets, these dangerous poets, or *I*s, a voice:

> How can I let them out?
> It is the noise that appalls me most of all,
> The unintelligible syllables.
> It is like a Roman mob,
> Small, taken one by one, but my god, together!
>
> I lay my ear to furious Latin.
> I am not a Caesar.
> I have simply ordered a box of maniacs.
> They can be sent back.
> They can die, I need feed them nothing, I am the owner.

In Hindu scripture, there is a story of the Ashvins, twin horsemen, who are the lords of light and are also honey-bearing, who along with drawing "white horses" and "ambrosial swans" wherever they go, also bring "honey to the bee" and prolong human life with the magic of the bee (its honey). Because of this, honey was also used in rituals, where people would sing:

Anoint me with the honey of the bee,
That I may speak forceful speech among men.

In Plath's poem "Stings," the *I* and a beekeeper visit the bee box full of bees, their "cheesecloth gauntlets neat and sweet" with their "thousand clean cells between us," and help to create for the bees the "hive itself" which is "a teacup," as she looks for the queen bee:

What am I buying, wormy mahogany?
Is there any queen at all in it?

Sure, of course, that "she is old" with "wings torn shawls," a "long body / Rubbed of its plush." Plath is sure that when she finds the queen, she will be so old and worn that she will be "unqueenly and even shameful."

And of course, there is the obvious comparison here. Sadly, many women, let alone female poets, feel that they are only as good as their youth and beauty. And that after their time of making is over, after they are old and grey, they are not useful to society anymore. They are not a queen to look for.

In a hive, the whole society is ruled by females. The job of male bees (the drones) is only to mate with the queen. How useless these drones must feel. What poems would they write.

The other bees in the hive are worker bees. They are all female and they make royal jelly to feed the queen larvae and if there is more than one queen who is hatched from this process, the multiple queens fight to the death until one queen is triumphant and becomes the queen bee.

In Plath's poem, as she wonders whether the queen bee she finds will be old, she converts herself into the queen bee, her queenly state unbeknownst to everyone as she "stand[s] in a column // Of winged, unmiraculous women, / Honey-drudgers. / I am no drudge."

Plath summons the queen bee, and her *I* becomes her, especially as she ends the poem:

> They thought death was worth it, but I
> Have a self to recover, a queen.
> Is she dead, is she sleeping?
> Where has she been,
> With her lion-red body, her wings of glass?
>
> Now she is flying
> More terrible than she ever was, red
> Scar in the sky, red comet
> Over the engine that killed her—
> The mausoleum, the wax house.

Plath's *I* has become the queen bee, has taken on her power and gone beyond the "women who only scurry, / Whose news is the open cherry, the open clover." She becomes the horrific thing, the shapeshifter bee monster who with unearthly bravado speaks for more than herself. Who has summoned the demon of the *duende*, trapped it like the Devil's horses, and rode it into the town square of the poem, smiling, a face full of brightly colored ribbons.

In the poem, Plath is not a worker bee, a drudge, meant to work and die with no great individual song. She is the queen bee and will make her book, the book this poem is in, her final book, *Ariel*. She writes:

It is almost over.
I am in control.
Here is my honey-machine,
It will work without thinking

As she takes on an identity of the queen bee, she will now "scour the creaming crests / As the moon, for its ivory powders, scours the sea," as a grand being, and make this poem, this book. By the end of the poem she uncovers the hive's queen bee, who is not willing to sting as a worker bee and die, but only to become queen, and only queen, not one of the worker bees, the drudges, the "winged, unmiraculous women," the worker females, those "women who only scurry, / Whose news is the open cherry, the open clover," the drudges whose only job is to go out to the fields and return to the hive, to serve the queen.

Instead by the end of the poem when she finds the queen, "her lion-red body, her wings of glass," "More terrible than she ever was, red / Scar in the sky, red comet," she finds her own red self—the persona of the poem who is in control, the queen poet that the hive (the book, other poets, all of poetry) must serve and submit to. She has a "terrible" power, and the poem's song, the swarm of it, brings it into being.

"The bees are flying. They taste the spring," Plath writes in the poem "Wintering." But bees fly because they must. Do poets write poems because they must? Bees and poets fly and write maybe because the spring is beautiful. It beckons with its soft fruits to the storage of sweet honey and beyond.

In "Stings," the beekeeper becomes the bee. So too, the poet becomes the poem. The hell that's all we've ever wanted. And still do.

We know from Plath's biography that her father was a beekeeper and this imagery is indebted to personal memory. And scholars have made much of this. But I don't think I should. And I don't think I will here.

A poet who writes with intense autobiography, who writes of unreal events and makes them real, writes in a high drama. Maybe this is what Plath did. The *I* of a poem is a place of high drama.

When I write about everyday events, things that have actually happened in my life, I am sure they have occurred, but I am also creating the hive of the poem and becoming the queen bee.

In a song called "Beez in the Trap," Nicki Minaj sings of being in a place of the highest power as a poet. She sings:

> Bitches ain't shit, and they ain't sayin' nothing
> A hundred mothafuckas can't tell me nothing
> I beez in the trap, bee-beez in the trap
> I beez in the trap, bee-beez in the trap

And of course, we are meant to realize that to be a bee is also to be a thing. It is the thing being been. Minaj plays with the words *be* and *being* as homophones of bees. Her *I* "beez," or exists, and plays on this grammatical variation on the word "am." Minaj is in the trap of being a poet. She beez in the trap. To be in this hell here with you, with all of us. All she's ever wanted. And still do.

In the first line of her song, she talks about all of the lesser poets singing today who "ain't sayin' nothing" because they "ain't shit." They have no mojo to bring to their *I*s and their songs, and subsequently their listeners. She goes on to say that even a "hundred" of them do not have the authority to sing as well as she does or to tell her what to do. Her *I* beez. It is, and it is not, it hates and loves, but more than anything, it has harnessed the *duende* and exists. Later she sings:

> If I weren't rappin' I'd be trappin'
> If I weren't trappin' I'd be pimpin'
> If weren't pimpin' I'd be gettin' it, period
> I don't smoke no bobby, but my denim be from Ricky
> Got your girl on molly and we smokin' loud and drinkin'
> Got my top back so you can see what I been thinkin'
> And if you know me then you know I've been thinkin' Franklin
> Money, thousands, True Religion trousers
> Got a private home, started from them public houses

Minaj's *I* tells a story of what it has overcome. It has started from "public houses," but by the sheer force of will, talent, intelligence, and strength of spirit, her *I* now has a "private home," "Money" in the "thousands" and expensive costumes, these "True Religion trousers." That no matter what, she would "be gettin' it, period," because of her superhuman swagger and muscle and her skill at making beautiful language. Minaj's *I* empowers her listeners, because when we hear her song, we feel all powerful, too. And it is only because she selflessly strips her *I* down bare to its nerve and is able to surround it with ineffable magic.

It's also important to mention that the word *beez* can be a person who sleeps around and is used in a derogatory way to signify a woman who has sex a lot, with many partners. Minaj undoubtedly is referencing this usage of the word, too, as a way to own this term and revive it with power and female empowerment.

And Minaj is the bee, but she also beezz and she also bees in the trap, the trap of being the singer meant to sing. The BE = BEEING after all.

Still, Plath's idea of being queen bee is in Nicki Minaj's idea of being. That to be a bee is to rule. Lorde, a young singer, in her song "Royals," sings to the audience that they should "Let me be your ruler, you can call me Queen Bee."

Lil' Kim, in her song "Came Back for You," sings to her fans, her real fans:

> Good evening ladies and gentlemen, I am the one and only Queen Bee
> After me there will be none, but you could call me Miss White
> Most people know me as Lil' Kim the head of the La Bella Mafia
> Oh, shoutout to my girl Victoria Gotti and the whole family stay up
>
> . . . .
>
> It's the real hip hop mami check the facts
> I'm sick of all you acts with your bubble gum raps
> Like the sand in the hourglass you out of your time
> Tried to go against the queen is you out of your mind?
> Even be at number two, your chances is slim
> Cause when God made Adam, he should've made Kim
> I gave a few passes but I never forget
> It's enough I got to put up with this Doo Doo Brown chick
> Now you and you wanna come at me from all sides
> I'm gettin money, don't think I just be lettin shit slide

In this song, she is the all-powerful poet, the queen. She lets her haters know she is boss and her fans know that she came from the dead to sing to them, to let them know she is their boss. To both haters and fans, she says she is here to stay. She is quieting the Roman mob—she is their ruler.

Rudolf Steiner talks about the work of worker bees and the queen bee. That their flight to collect pollen and turn it into honey is a marriage flight. I think that this is a moment of high drama, too. He explains that the worker bees visit the flowers and the trees, but that they are children of the sun, just like the queen. And that their lives are governed by the length of time it takes for the sun to rotate on its axis (a length of time he said was twenty-one days, even though now we know otherwise).

I think that when the poet is a queen bee she speaks to her workers, but she also speaks for the sun. The queen bee is not like her workers. Like Plath says, "They thought death was worth it, but I / Have a self to recover, a queen." The *I* of the poet will always be the bee that is called back into the poem. The *I* is the bee that is called back, in a "lion-red body" with "her wings of glass."

The worker bees live to visit the flowers and trees. Their marriage flight is in the swarm and in the drama of the swarm. They are the children of the sun, as is the queen. But they are governed by the laws of the sun. The queen bee is governed by the laws of the swarm, which is the poem. The marriage flight she makes is with the self—there is no one like her. The flowers and trees come to her through being. And she is governed only by being the only one of her kind. The sun speaks through her. And sun and queen bee are the song of it all.

Such sovereignty. Such eternal dignity we see in bees. We hear this ring of unearthly claim in their song.

How does the song go? That bees do it, that birds do it. Bees do it. Birds do it.

The literary goddess Chris Kraus has a song she sings when the bees have gotten too much for her. She said she made it up when she was taking a hike and all of these bees swarmed her and she sang to them:

Oh bees, please
Oh bees, please
Leave us in peace

Or this is how she typed out the song to me, as when I told her I was writing this lecture, she offered this song. When I told my friend Robbie Dewhurst about this song, he told me once he and Chris were in her garden and all of these bees swarmed them and they had to run inside like mad people. And now as I write this down to you, Robbie has recently become a bee husbander.

But when the bees swarmed them in her garden, Chris offered her bee song to them. And when she wrote me about it, she said that she would sing it to me, too, and then she did the next time I saw her. And the song was sweet and sinister, and she repeated the last line, so that the song is really:

Oh bees, please
Oh bees, please
Leave us in peace
Leave us in peace

Maybe she didn't need to write that last line twice when she sent it to me initially. Maybe when you write a poem, you can just write once what in person you might repeat. Maybe the notation of the poem is the intricate container of wax that can then fly away when you choose to leave the hive of the words.

Sammy Davis Jr. has a song called "The Candy Man," and in the song the Candy Man is very powerful. He's all-powerful. The song asks us:

> Who can take a sunrise
> Sprinkle it with dew
> Cover it with choc'late and a miracle or two
> The Candy Man
> Oh, the Candy Man can

I forgot to say earlier that I started thinking seriously about the movie *Candyman* when I found a copy of its screenplay in a used bookstore. But the screenplay was the notation for the movie, was the hive of the song. On the cover of the screenplay was a honeycomb.

Of course that story has always been about the bees. I think the convergence of self and other is a kind of forgiveness only the hum can bring. Maybe divine love is the forgiveness that a poet must be the bee to survive, but also must sing the bee song to sing.

May Swenson has a love poem called "Four-Word Lines," in which the desire to be a flower pollinated by a bee is all a lover can hope for:

> Your eyes are just
> like bees, and I
> feel like a flower.

Their brown power makes
a breeze go over
my skin. When your
lashes ride down and
rise like brown bees'
legs, your pronged gaze
makes my eyes gauze.
I wish we were
in some shade and
no swarm of other
eyes to know that
I'm a flower breathing
bare, laid open to
your bees' warm stare.
I'd let you wade
in me and seize
with your eager brown
bees' power a sweet
glistening at my core.

And of course this sexual sublimity is what a flower might want, but a poet is not a flower, it's a bee, a real bee bloomed in real water. And Swenson knows that, so really even though she asks the *you* to be her bee, she turns into a bee herself in the act of loving, with her "eyes gauze," her bee eyes.

Book Four of Virgil's *Georgics* is all about bees. First it uses bees as a kind of model of how humans should be—that they should work for the society and the greater good. Later in the book, Aristaeus loses his bees, and tries to get them back by blinding a seer, but it doesn't work, because he has angered too many nymphs. And Proteus tells him his real crime was to kill Eurydice, the true love of Orpheus, who lost her twice to death and now must sing and long forever, instead of having completeness.

The end of the book is about the life of being a poet. You sing for the thing not even imaginable in your grasp. You are not the army man, as Virgil writes, who holds victory in the body. Your body is a corpse always, beneath the beech tree. You rule the world only in the aftermath, in the spaces between the real and the living.

Harold Acton, a poet and writer from the twentieth century, wrote of a poem that it was "as keen as a bee." Maybe the keenness of a bee is what all poems strive for.

Love, like devotion to a God, is sweet. The Candy Man can make the everyday into candy. The bee can take a flower, who is destined to die, and make the immortal liquid that can cure anything, that can make the unsinging sing again. The poet, too, can do a lot. But the poem cannot cure the unseen from its seeing. It must be and being. There is no peace.

INTUITION, THE ECHO OF THE FUTURE

Perhaps bees—a swarm of bees—are related to intuition. Maybe that's what ghosts are. Maybe that's what poems do.

What is the feeling we feel when we know something is amiss. Is it just chance or do we really know something? Is life about finding our mystical opposites and forgiveness, forgiving ourselves in another dimension, creating the comb and the hive? And when we know the spiritual other, do we forgive it still through song?

Being a poet is about telepathy and intuition. It's about knowing things that you can't know you know. Have you ever had that experience when reading a poem, that the poem knows you? I have. It has happened when reading and writing a poem. Sometimes I have written things within a poem that I couldn't have known would come true years later. What part of me knew? Was it my swarm self, in another space, that spoke to me through song?

What is the swarm of bees that enters a poem when language is created? What is the radio the poet is tapping into with its gentle hum? It is the thing of being, moving around and absorbing energy.

Several years ago, in a summer writing program in Amherst, I met a fantastic poet named Lynn Houston, who had, for an entire cycle already, raised a family of bees. She didn't know that I was thinking about bees and poetry so much when she told our group about queens and wild queens, when she discussed her "babies" as a group of female warriors kept in a hive. Maybe she did or did not know, in those moments when she recounted to me about the bees, that she belonged to a lineage of great, wild, wild women. We were poets. All of us.

A bit into her bee stories, Lynn described how she had recently found out she was deathly allergic to bee stings and had almost died when a swarm attacked her. She said she was feeding the bees and had not suited up properly because she was in a hurry, and the bees kind of flipped out, thinking that their queen was in danger, and after a few seconds all came at her and stung her, hundreds of them, and she went into shock and narrowly survived the attack.

What struck me in her story was the way she described the sounds of her bees and how these sounds changed when they were about to attack. She described the normal hum when bees are happy in the hive, then how they shift to a louder tone, and then to a screeching sound when they are about to attack, which in my imagination sounds like a scene in a traditional horror film, when the murderer has come into the room with a knife and sets it in the air to stab you. Maybe I was thinking of the shower scene in *Psycho* a bit, yet the swarm of knives seems even so much more sinister.

In a conference paper called "Silent Summer" Lynn gave at the Western Literature Association Conference in Berkeley during the fall of 2013, she described these very sounds more eloquently than I could even begin to, so I will share some of her writing with you now:

> Bees make noise through the vibration of their wings. When you approach a healthy hive of bees, you hear a hum. A sound that ends in an "m"—emmm. This is their tranquil, resting, go-about-their-business noise. It becomes even duller at night, just the letter "m"—mmmm—when most of them retreat deep in the hive. Once you get close enough to the hive, guard bees that stand along the entrance will spot you and begin a new sound that is picked up by the rest of the hive, a song that warns of a potential intruder. That's when the "b" and "z" sounds start—"bzzss" which can rise to the same sound ending in a sharper staccato "t" if you make more movements to approach—"bsstt." This is often the sound the bees make as you open up the hive, expose it to the sun, and begin examining the frames. Eventually, sooner if you jar or knock any of the hive furniture, the disturbance to the hive increases the pitch to almost a siren, an "errr" sound, aggressive. At this point, bees begin to fly around you and land on you trying to find a vulnerable place to attack this intruder to their home. Your movements, smell, and exhalation of breath, if not controlled, could convince them that you mean harm, at which point the guard bees fly straight into your face with a very high pitched "reee."

Of course it is the *bsstt* and *reee* a person would need to look out for, before it was too late. But maybe it would be too late. Maybe it is the *bzzss* that are the worst, because things are about to get bad. And is this where we get the buzz of buzzing bees from? Do we ever, as humans, hear the hum? Or is every sound of a bee a battle cry, calling out to the wild for the brethren, in search of solidarity and aid?

And how do the bees speak to one another, to communicate when it is time to worry, and to attack? It isn't intuition that they speak together—it is sound. But are these things one and the same? I do not know.

I mentioned the bees in Virgil's *Georgics* a bit earlier. Even in their glory, there is no escape from the poison darts, the bees' anger, the poets' strikes. He writes:

> There's no end to the wrath of bees—vexed, they'll inflame their stings
> with poison and, fastening to a vein, deposit darts that you can't see—
> inflicting harm, they'll forfeit their own lives. . . .
> The more trials sent to test them, the keener they become, one and all,
> to throw themselves into the mending of their tumbled world.

Perhaps here, too, Virgil makes the bee akin to a poet. After all, it is a poet who also becomes keener with the more trials sent to test them. The more a poet has to translate emotion, and thought, into language, the sharper their ability to do it again and better the next time. The best poems are the ones a poet is just about to write.

Fifteen years ago now, I taught some third graders in a Writers in the Schools program. We were reading W.S. Merwin together, and when we read his poem "Vixen" during class, the children noticed that he did not use punctuation. It was probably in that moment that I decided to use as little punctuation as possible in my poems. Merwin did this to create poems that spring off the page. Maybe he did it, too, to let the poems be bees, free and wild from their honeycomb.

Merwin's poem "The River of Bees" describes a swarm of them, come to speak through intuitive forces and the dreamworld:

> In a dream I returned to the river of bees
> Five orange trees by the bridge and
> Beside two mills my house
> Into whose courtyard a blind man followed
> The goats and stood singing
> Of what was older
>
> Soon it will be fifteen years
>
> He was old he will have fallen into his eyes
>
> I took my eyes
> A long way to the calendars
> Room after room asking how shall I live
>
> One of the ends is made of streets
> One man processions carry through it
> Empty bottles their
> Image of hope
> It was offered to me by name
>
> Once once and once
> In the same city I was born
> Asking what shall I say
>
> He will have fallen into his mouth
> Men think they are better than grass

I return to his voice rising like a forkful of hay

He was old he is not real nothing is real
Nor the noise of death drawing water

We are the echo of the future

On the door it says what to do to survive
But we were not born to survive
Only to live

This poem reverberates with the Eric Baus poem I discussed earlier. Merwin exclaims toward the end of the poem that the man he describes "is not real" and "nothing is real." Baus exclaims something awful in his poem, too, as he writes, "Flowers are not real. Bees are not real. Water is not real." In Merwin's poem, we see a man who is actually blind follow the sound of bees into the day, obliterated by the beauty of nature (the "Five orange trees") that he may or may not be able to see, but can intuit—he knows it, he goes into it. Merwin reminds us in his poem that we are not real and this is because we were not meant to be. We are meant "Only to live," and that in itself is not a reality, because the physical existences we get so used to in bodies are endlessly changing, until the alchemy of death renders them into a form that is so unlike what is familiar as a human being, it must not be real at all.

Merwin also writes, "We are the echo of the future." I think that this is a very real thing. In a poem, we echo what will already be. Maybe we make what will be by being it already through language. Whatever the case, the man in Merwin's poem is always me, because I can read it. The man is Merwin, too. And he is you, too. Because when the bees *reee* they speak for all of us, to warn of the impending end we all face, but we face it with bitter breath together, in a neverending song.

In "To make a prairie," Dickinson writes:

> To make a prairie it takes a clover and one bee,
> One clover, and a bee,
> And revery.
> The revery alone will do,
> If bees are few.

I've always thought that in this poem, she means to say that you can make an expansive space of nature, you can make in your mind a wide-open field of flowers and being, with just one clover and a bee and, of course, "revery." But by the end of this short poem, we learn that in the absence of bees, you must have daydreaming, you must have revery. And in such a short time, she shows us that bees and daydreaming are somehow the same—that bees make dreams appear.

In a letter to her sister-in-law, Susie Gilbert, from the winter of 1853, Dickinson writes:

> How fast we will have to talk then—there will be those farewell gaieties—and all the days before, of which I have had no fact, and there will be your absence, and your *presence*, my Susie dear, sweetest, and brightest, and best of every and all the themes. *It is sweet* to talk, dear Susie, with those whom God has given us, lest we should be alone—and you and I have *tasted it*, and found it *very sweet*; even as fragrant flowers, o'er which the bee hums and lingers, and hums *more* for the lingering.
>
> I find it very lonely, to part with *one of mine*, with mine *especially*, and the days will have more *hours* while you are gone away.

Susan Gilbert was married to Dickinson's brother, Austin. Many scholars believe Susie was the love of Dickinson's life and her muse; she showed more of her poems to Susie than to any other human being. She lived across Dickinson's lawn in her brother's house her entire married life, and Dickinson called again and again to her in letters like this one.

Whatever the true nature of Dickinson's emotions, one can feel the aching Dickinson expresses to Gilbert, as she writes of her "presence" which is the "sweetest, and brightest," and so "very sweet; even as fragrant flowers, o'er which the bee hums and lingers, and hums more for the lingering."

Just like many of the other poets I have discussed in this lecture, Dickinson makes the work of a poet akin to a bee's. For just as the bee lingers more over the sweetest flowers and gives off in sound a (non-threatening) hum, a poet too in the midst of beauty sings more in the space of it, not to survive, because that's not the point, but to live. The bees talking. The sweetest bees.

Walt Whitman, in "Specimen Days," writes of bumblebees:

> May-month—month of swarming, singing, mating birds—the bumble-bee month—month of the flowering lilac—(and then my own birth-month.)

And he writes of the sensual overload of nature and living, and because he is a poet, he feels to record this overload with his characteristic and large, undulating detail:

> The blue birds, grass birds and robins, in every direction. . . .
>
> . . . the croaking of the pond frogs and the first white of the dog-wood blossoms. Now the golden dandelions in endless profusion, spotting the ground everywhere. The white cherry and pear-blows—the wild violets . . .

But it is the bees that capture his poet heart with their metaphysical kinship. As he writes, the bees are "conveying to me a new and pronounc'd sense of strength, beauty, vitality and movement" with the

> deep musical drone of these bees, flitting, balancing, darting to and fro about me by hundreds—big fellows with light yellow jackets, great glistening swelling bodies, stumpy heads and gauzy wings—humming their perpetual rich mellow boom. (Is there not a hint in it for a musical composition, of which it should be the back-ground? some bumble-bee symphony?). . . .
>
> . . . these wild bees, whose loud and steady humming makes an undertone to the whole, and to my mood and the hour.

For Whitman, it is the hum of the bees that makes them like the poet, with the gift of musical composition, of song. They are overwhelmingly strong, beautiful, and vital, with immense mojo. They have magic in their song, creating a symphony with their loud and steady humming, with their overwhelming power, which overtakes even a wild garden in spring. In their incessant undertone, they overtake everything.

Whitman's "Give Me the Splendid, Silent Sun," a love poem about the fall and Manhattan, talks of bees:

> Keep your splendid, silent sun;
> Keep your woods, O Nature, and the quiet places by the woods;
> Keep your fields of clover and timothy, and your corn-fields and or-chards;
> Keep the blossoming buckwheat fields, where the Ninth-month bees hum;
> Give me faces and streets! give me these phantoms incessant and endless along the trottoirs!
> Give me interminable eyes! give me women! give me comrades and lovers by the thousand!
> Let me see new ones every day! let me hold new ones by the hand every day!
> Give me such shows! give me the streets of Manhattan!
> Give me Broadway, with the soldiers marching—give me the sound of the trumpets and drums!
> (The soldiers in companies or regiments—some, starting away, flush'd and reckless;
> Some, their time up, returning, with thinn'd ranks—young, yet very old, worn, marching, noticing nothing;)
> —Give me the shores and the wharves heavy-fringed with the black ships!
> O such for me! O an intense life! O full to repletion, and varied!
> The life of the theatre, bar-room, huge hotel, for me!
> The saloon of the steamer! the crowded excursion for me! the torch-light procession!

The dense brigade, bound for the war, with high piled military wagons
following;
People, endless, streaming, with strong voices, passions, pageants;
Manhattan streets, with their powerful throbs, with the beating drums,
as now;
The endless and noisy chorus, the rustle and clank of muskets, (even
the sight of the wounded;)
Manhattan crowds, with their turbulent musical chorus—with varied
chorus, and light of the sparkling eyes;
Manhattan faces and eyes forever for me.

Whitman mentions the "Ninth-month bees" in the space of a bright day and within the "endless and noisy chorus" of the "Manhattan crowds" that he loves with their "turbulent musical chorus—with varied chorus," their gorgeous urban hum.

These "Ninth-month bees" are so odd—they seem not of this world, and I, for one, am not sure what "Ninth-month" is supposed to mean. I think it means September—that this walk is the end of summer, as newness of sun is silent and diminishing. These bees are old.

I also think of course of childbirth and the gestation of a human baby. In the ninth month the baby as a being inside the womb is over and it must be born, but also be reborn in a way. It is entering the world in the form that we can fathom it as living humans, but it has already lived an entire lifetime as a being inside the hive of its mother's womb. It dies, in a way, to be born and with us.

I once did Elizabeth Kray's fabulous Walt Whitman walking tour of historic New York City. I learned so much about Whitman on that day. Kray had us go through several locations on Broadway that most of us (especially the seasoned New Yorkers) might have taken for granted, regular old bodegas and shops. In one particularly interesting part of the tour, we stopped in front of Victoria's Secret on Broadway, which used to be a brothel. I can't tell you how much it delights me to encounter this Victoria's Secret now and to know this "secret" to this day.

What I really learned in the tour was something else about the sound and length of Whitman's lines that Kray may or may not have intended me to uncover. Part of the tour has you walk along until you get to Brooklyn. It is a relatively long walk and one that Whitman did almost daily. While walking along, I had an almost mystical experience and heard not just the sound of the cars and people along the road, but the horse-drawn carriages of Whitman's day, the "endless and noisy chorus." Suddenly I realized why his lines were long and extended seemingly on and on. The walk, like poetry, like Manhattan, had no end. The bees' song was an endless, splendid spring we must walk along. And it's an honor to make this walk my lifeline.

John Keats, in an 1818 letter to his friend John Hamilton Reynolds, writes of the bees:

> It has been an old comparison for our urging on—the Beehive; however, it seems to me that we should rather be the flower than the Bee—for it is a false notion that more is gained by receiving than giving—no, the receiver and the giver are equal in their benefits. The flower, I doubt not, receives a fair guerdon from the Bee—its leaves blush deeper in the next spring—and who shall say between man and woman which is the most delighted? Now it is more noble to sit like Jove than to fly like Mercury—let us not therefore go hurrying about and collecting honey, bee-like buzzing here and there impatiently from a knowledge of what is to be arrived at; but let us open our leaves like a flower and be passive and receptive—budding patiently under the eye of Apollo and taking hints from

> every noble insect that favours us with a visit—sap will be given us for meat and dew for drink. I was led into these thoughts, my dear Reynolds, by the beauty of the morning operating on a sense of Idleness—I have not read any books—the Morning said I was right—I had no idea but of the morning, and the thrush said I was right . . .

It seems as if Keats might agree with Dickinson's poem, that bees are related to revery, as he seems to favor the scene of bees and flowers, and the "sense of Idleness" of daydreams, which make poetry.

Still, he seems to favor the passive work of a flower to that of a bee. The bee actively collects pollen, but Keats thinks that it is better to accept what the world gives as knowledge. To not seek it out as a master of knowledge, but as receiver.

I think that he is right in part. A poet must listen to the radio waves of this world and the next one and respond through poetry. It's true. But I think the poet must be more than the flower. He must be the bee—with all its valor, to leave the inside and seek the truth.

James Schuyler, in "Hymn to Life," writes:

> Through it all the forsythia begins to bloom, brown
> And yellow and warm as lit gas jets, clinging like bees to
> The arching canes where starlings take cover from foraging cats. Not
> To know: what have these years of living and being lived taught us?
> Not to quarrel? Scarcely. You want to shoot pool, I want to go home

I think I prefer Schuyler's relationship to the bees to Keats's. After all, being a bee and a flower is about living, and "what have these years of living and being lived taught us" anyway. There is strife everywhere. Even in our most intimate relationships, we don't share the same goals—"You want to shoot pool. I want to go home." As people, we don't move as bees, all knowing what we are meant to do—to mate the queen, to protect the queen, to be the queen, to be a wild queen.

No, Schuyler would not like to come back to life as a flower. He wants to come back into his voice as a bee. After all, orange flowers, the bees—none of it is real. Only the voice, the sound is real. Replace everything else for sound, the poems tell us.

THE GREY ROOM

In "The Room of My Life," Anne Sexton describes the "room of [her] life" where the "objects keep changing," but all hang "like a cave of bees" that she feels and feeds as its own "world." It is in this room, with its endless pit of bees, that "the sea . . . bangs in [her] throat."

My favorite poems are the ones with broken lyrics and gut-wrenching, imaginative realism. I think it is because too they make me think of bees. Because a bee's life is broken, just from the start of it.

Everyone knows that the events in poems are real and then aren't, too. Even if they happened—that doesn't mean they are real. Most readers of poems don't have the privilege of knowing the difference—if the poem means something and lasts, they won't know the poet as a real person, just an abstraction—a set of black type on page or sound wavelength on recording. That's it. So, is the plight of a poet for naught? Oh, I don't think so. What's most important to a poem is real pain (and pain can be sweet). It has to feel real. (Whatever that means.) And I think that poems that *feel* real are somehow beyond the real.

What is the pure being that is the poet that writes the poem? It is never pure. It never speaks from a pure place. It is the monster in the poem with a confusing set of emotions, based in real love and real hate.

It is a swarm of bees, flying everywhere. After all, not everyone is aware there is a demon-queen living inside each of us. But the poet knows. The demon fractures the self. Into its mystical opposites. It does it for the love of you.

Dear reader, the pure me loves you. Remember: "The bees are flying. They taste the spring."

You know I've always loved you. We lived as one in dreams.

And I'll come back again to tell you so.

Just watch me.

SELECTED BIBLIOGRAPHY & WORKS CITED

Agamben, Giorgio. *The Open: Man and Animal*. Palo Alto, CA: Stanford University Press, 2004.

Ascher, Rodney, dir. *Room 237*. Los Angeles: Highland Park Classics, 2013.

Bagayoko, Amadou, Manu Chao, and Mariam Doumbia. "Sénégal Fast Food." On *Dimanche à Bamako*. New York: Sony ATV Music Publishing, 2004.

Barry, Dan. "In the Wilds of New Jersey, A Legend Inspires a Hunt." *New York Times*, September 7, 2008.

Batchelor, David. *Chromophobia*. London: Reaktion Books, 2000.

Baus, Eric. *Tuned Droves*. Portland, OR: Octopus Books, 2008.

Blair, David. *Wax, or the Discovery of Television Among the Bees*. Las Vegas: David Blair Productions and Mainz, Germany: Zweites Deutsches Fernsehen (ZDF), 1991.

Blake, William. *The Complete Poems*. Edited by Alicia Ostriker. New York: Penguin, 1977.

Boswell, James. *The Life of Samuel Johnson*. New York: Penguin, 2008.

Bricusse, Leslie, and Anthony Newley. "The Candy Man." Sammy Davis Jr. On *Sammy Davis Jr. Now*. Culver City, CA: MGM Studios, 1972.

Buckingham, Lindsey. "Tusk." Fleetwood Mac. On *Tusk*. Los Angeles: Warner Brothers, 1979.

Carroll, Lewis. *Through the Looking-Glass and What Alice Found There*. New York: The Macmillan Company, 1899.

Celan, Paul. *Paul Celan: Selections*. Translated by Jerome Rothenberg. Oakland, CA: University of California Press, 2005.

Derrida, Jacques. *The Animal That Therefore I Am*. New York: Fordham University Press, 2009.

———. *Between the Blinds: A Derrida Reader*. Edited by Peggy Kamuf. New York: Columbia University Press, 1991.

Diane, Alela, and Tom Menig. "Of Many Colors." On *Alela Diane and Wild Divine*. London: Rough Trade Records, 2011.

Dickinson, Emily. *The Letters of Emily Dickinson*. Edited by Thomas H. Johnson. Cambridge, MA: The Belknap Press of Harvard University Press, 1986.

———. *The Poems of Emily Dickinson*. Edited by R. W. Franklin. Cambridge, MA: The Belknap Press of Harvard University Press, 1999.

Donaldson, Walter, and Gus Kahn. "Love Me Or Leave Me." Nina Simone. On *Little Girl Blue*. New York: Bethlehem Records, 1958.

Doolittle, Hilda. *Notes on Thought and Vision*. San Francisco: City Lights, 2001.

———. *Collected Poems, 1912–1944*. New York: New Directions Publishing, 1982.

Doty, Mark. *Dog Years: A Memoir*. New York: HarperCollins, 2009.

Epps, Tauheed, Onika Tanya Maraj, and Maurice Jordan. "Beez in the Trap." Nicki Minaj. On *Pink Friday: Roman Reloaded*. Santa Monica, CA: Universal Republic Records, 2012.

Fallon, Peter. *Virgil: Georgics*. Oxford: Oxford University Press, 2004.

Ferry, David. *Gilgamesh: A New Rendering in English Verse*. New York: Farrar, Straus and Giroux, 1992.

———. *The Odes of Horace*. New York: Farrar, Straus and Giroux, 1997.

García Lorca, Federico. *In Search of Duende*. Edited by Christopher Maurer. New York: New Directions, 2010.

Gass, William. *On Being Blue*. Boston: David R. Godine, Inc., 1975.

Goethe, Johann Wolfgang von. *Theory of Colours*. Translated by Charles Eastlake. London: John Murray, 1840.

Graham, Lanier F., ed. *The Rainbow Book: A Collection of Essays and Illustrations*

Devoted to Rainbows in Particular and Spectral Sequences in General. New York: Random House, 1975.

Greene, Maxine. *Releasing the Imagination: Essays on Education, the Arts, and Social Change*. San Francisco: Jossey-Bass, Inc., 1995.

Grice, Gordon. *The Book of Deadly Animals*. New York: Penguin Books, 2012.

Hall, Daryl, and John Oates. "Sara Smile." On *Daryl Hall & John Oates*. Los Angeles: Warner/Chappell Music, Inc., 1975.

Houston, Lynn. "Silent Summer." Western Literature Association Conference, Berkeley, CA, fall 2013.

Jabès, Edmond. *The Book of Questions* (Volume II). Translated by Rosmarie Waldrop. Middletown, CT: Wesleyan University Press, 1991.

Jacobs, Ken, dir. *"Slow is Beauty"—Rodin*. The Apparition Theater of New York, 1974.

Jones, Kimberly, Christopher Wallace, Jimmy L. Webb, and Kanye Omari West. "Came Back for You." Lil' Kim. On *La Bella Mafia*. New York: Atlantic Records, 2003.

Kapil, Bhanu. *Humanimal: A Project for Future Children*. Berkeley: Kelsey Street Press, 2009.

Keats, John. *Letters of John Keats to His Family and Friends*. London/New York: MacMillan and Co., 1891.

Kierkegaard, Søren. *Fear and Trembling*. Translated by Alistair Hanney. New York: Penguin, 1986.

Kubrick, Stanley, dir. *The Shining*. Written by Stanley Kubrick and Diane Johnson (screenplay), based on the novel by Stephen King. Los Angeles: Warner Brothers, 1980.

Lawrence, David Herbert. *The Complete Poems of D. H. Lawrence*. New York: Penguin, 1983.

Mayer, Bernadette. *A Bernadette Mayer Reader*. New York: New Directions, 1992.

Merwin, W. S. *Migration: New and Selected Poems*. Port Townsend, WA: Copper Canyon Press, 2005.

Metzger, Elizabeth. *The Spirit Papers*. Amherst, MA: The University of Massachusetts Press, 2017.

Neitzsche, Friedrich Wilhelm. *Selected Letters of Friedrich Nietzsche*. Edited and translated by Christopher Middleton. Cambridge, MA: Hackett Publishing, 1996.

Nelson, Maggie. *The Art of Cruelty: A Reckoning*. New York: W. W. Norton, 2011.

———. *Bluets*. Seattle: Wave Books, 2009.

Notley, Alice. *Certain Magical Acts*. New York: Penguin, 2016.

———. *Grave of Light: New and Selected Poems, 1970–2005*. Middletown, CT: Wesleyan University Press, 2008.

Paz, Octavio. *The Double Flame: Love and Eroticism*. Translated by Helen Lane. Ontario, FL: Harcourt, Inc., 1993.

Plath, Sylvia. *Ariel*. New York: Harper and Row, 1966.

Ransome, Hilda M. *The Sacred Bee in Ancient Times and Folklore*. New York: Dover Publishing, Inc., 2004.

Rimbaud, Arthur. *Arthur Rimbaud: Complete Works*. Translated by Paul Schmidt. New York: Harper Perennial Modern Classics, 2008.

Rose, Bernard, dir. *Candyman*. Written by Clive Barker and Bernard Rose. Los Angeles: Propaganda Films & PolyGram Filmed Entertainment, 1992.

Sagan, Carl. *Cosmos*. New York: Random House, 1980; New York: Ballantine, 2013.

Sanders, Jay, curator. *Rituals of Rented Island: Object Theater, Loft Performance, and the New Psychodrama—Manhattan, 1970–1980*. Exhibit at the Whitney Museum of American Art, October 31, 2013–February 2, 2014.

Sappho. *If Not, Winter: Fragments of Sappho*. Translated by Anne Carson. New York: Vintage, 2003.

Sartre, Jean-Paul. *The Imaginary*. Translated by Jonathan Webber. New York: Routledge, 2004.

Schuyler, James. *Collected Poems*. New York: Farrar, Straus and Giroux, 1993.

Sexton, Anne. *The Complete Poems*. New York: Houghton Mifflin Harcourt, 1981.

———. *45 Mercy Street*. Edited by Linda Grey Sexton. New York: Houghton Mifflin Harcourt, 1976.

Shelley, Mary Wollstonecraft. *Frankenstein, or The Modern Prometheus*. London: Dent, 1869.

Spicer, Jack. *The House That Jack Built: The Collected Lectures of Jack Spicer*. Edited by Peter Gizzi. Middletown, CT: Wesleyan University Press, 1998.

Stein, Gertrude. *The Geographical History of America*. Baltimore, MD: The Johns Hopkins University Press, 1936.

———. *Tender Buttons*. London: Dover Publications, 1997.

Steiner, Rudolf. *Nine Lectures on Bees Given in 1923 to the Workmen at the Goetheanum*. Translated by Marna Pease and Carl Alexander Mier. Blauvelt, NY: Rudolf Steiner Publications, 1964.

Stevens, Wallace. *The Collected Poems of Wallace Stevens*. New York: Alfred A. Knopf, 1990.

———. *Harmonium*. New York: A. A. Knopf, 1931.

Stewart, George R., Jr. "Color and Science in Poetry," *The Scientific Monthly*, Vol. 30, No. 1 (Jan., 1930), pp. 71–78.

Swenson, May. *The Complete Love Poems of May Swenson*. New York: Houghton Mifflin Harcourt, 1991.

Tammet, Daniel. *Born on a Blue Day*. New York: Simon and Schuster, 2007.

Trakl, Georg. *The Last Gold of Expired Stars: Complete Poems (1908–1914)*. Translated by Jim Doss and Werner Schmitt. Baltimore, MD: Loch Raven Press, 2011.

Vendler, Helen. *Dickinson: Selected Poems and Commentaries*. Cambridge, MA: The Belknap Press of Harvard University Press, 2010.

Weiner, Hannah. *The Fast*. Berkeley, CA: United Artists Books, 1992.

Whitman, Walt. *Poems of Walt Whitman (Leaves of Grass)*. New York: T. Y. Crowell & Co., 1902.

———. *Specimen Days & Collect*. Philadelphia, PA: Rees Welsh and Company, 1882.

Wieners, John. *Supplication: Selected Poems*. Edited by Robert Dewhurst (with Joshua Beckman and CAConrad). Seattle: Wave Books, 2015.

Williams, William Carlos. *The Collected Poems: Volume I, 1909–1939*. New York: New Directions, 1986.

Wittgenstein, Ludwig. *Remarks on Colour.* Translated by Linda L. McAlister and Margarete Schättle. Berkeley: University of California Press, 1977.

Yelich-O'Connor, Ella Marija Lani (Lorde), and Joel Little. "Royals." Lorde. On *Pure Heroine*. Santa Monica, CA: Universal Music Group, 2012.

ACKNOWLEDGMENTS

The Bagley Wright Lecture Series on Poetry supports contemporary poets as they explore in depth their own thinking on poetry and poetics and give a series of lectures resulting from these investigations.

This work evolved from lectures given at the following institutions: "Poetry and the Metaphysical I," Harvard University, Cambridge, MA, October 10, 2013; "On the Materiality of the Imagination," Seattle Arts and Lectures, Seattle, WA, November 21, 2013; "The Beast: How Poetry Makes Us Human," Library of Congress, Washington, DC, December 5, 2013; "Poetry and the Metaphysical I," University of California–Riverside, Palm Desert, CA, December 2013; "What Is Color in Poetry or Is It the Wild Wind in the Space of the Word," The Poetry Foundation, Chicago, IL, January 23, 2014; "On the Materiality of the Imagination," the Renaissance Society at the University of Chicago, January 31, 2014. "JSTOR presents: Spectres, Traces, Phantoms, and Sparks: A Poetry Séance by Dorothea Lasky," Morbid Anatomy Museum, Brooklyn, NY, April 2016; "The Beast: How Poetry Makes Us Human," in conjunction with some writing exercises at A Public Space, November 26, 2016.

Thank you to Christina Davis at Harvard University, Rebecca Hoogs at Seattle Arts and Lectures, Rob Casper at the Library of Congress, Anthony McCann at University of California–Riverside/Palm Desert, Stephen Young at the Poetry Foundation, Hamza Walker at the Renaissance Society, Cathy Halley at the Morbid Anatomy Museum, and Brett Fletcher Lauer at A Public Space, and their respective staffs, for welcoming the Bagley Wright Lecture Series into their programming, and for collaborating on scheduling, promoting, introducing, and recording these events. The Series would be impossible without such partners.

by the Estate of Sylvia Plath. Editorial material copyright © 1981 by Ted Hughes. Reprinted by permission of HarperCollins Publishers. "Cigarettes and Whiskey and Wild, Wild Women" from *45 Mercy Street* by Anne Sexton, edited by Linda Gray Sexton. Copyright © 1976 by Linda Gray Sexton and Loring Conant, Jr., Executors of the Estate of Anne Sexton. Reprinted by permission of Houghton Mifflin Harcourt Publishing Company. All rights reserved. "Poetry Is a Destructive Force," copyright 1942 by Wallace Stevens, copyright renewed 1970 by Holly Stevens; from *The Collected Poems of Wallace Stevens* by Wallace Stevens. Used by permission of Alfred A. Knopf, an imprint of the Knopf Doubleday Publishing Group, a division of Penguin Random House LLC. All rights reserved. "Orange Water" by Eric Baus, originally published in *Tuned Droves* (Octopus Books, 2008) and used by permission of the author. Lyrics from "Beez in the Trap" and "Came Back for You" appear courtesy of Hal Leonard. "Four-Word Lines" from *The Complete Love Poems of May Swenson*. Copyright © 1991, 2003 by The Literary Estate of May Swenson. Reprinted by permission of Houghton Mifflin Harcourt Publishing Company. All rights reserved. W. S. Merwin, "The River of Bees" from *Migration: New and Selected Poems*. Copyright © 1967, 2005 by W. S. Merwin. Reprinted with the permission of The Permissions Company, Inc. on behalf of Copper Canyon Press, www.coppercanyonpress.org. Also used with permission of Bloodaxe Books, Hexham, UK. Emily Dickinson's letter to Susan Gilbert excerpted from *The Letters of Emily Dickinson*, edited by Thomas H. Johnson, Associate Editor, Theodora Ward, Cambridge, Mass.: The Belknap Press of Harvard University Press, Copyright © 1958 by the President and Fellows of Harvard College. Copyright © renewed 1986 by the President and Fellows of Harvard College. Copyright © 1914, 1924, 1932, 1942 by Martha Dickinson Bianchi. Copyright © 1952 by Alfred Leete Hampson. Copyright © 1960 by Mary L. Hampson. Used with permission.

NOTE FROM THE AUTHOR

Thank you to the editors who published earlier versions of these works: "A Belief in Ghosts: Poetry and the Shared Imagination," Arts & Culture, *JSTOR Daily*, October 2016; "Poetry and The Metaphysical I," *Wave Composition*, September 2015; "What Is Color in Poetry or Is It the Wild Wind in the Space of the Word," *Poetry*, Fall 2014.

Thank you to everyone at the Bagley Wright Lecture Series for inviting me to be a part of this series and for making this book come to life. Thank you to the Wave Books editors, Joshua Beckman, Heidi Broadhead, and Matthew Zapruder, for all of their care and aid in the writing of this book. Thank you always to my friends and family for their endless love and support.